CONTEXTS

Series Editor:

Steven Matthews
Oxford Brookes University, UK

Other titles in the series

MODERNISM

STEVEN MATTHEWS

Oxford Brookes University, UK

A member of the Hodder Headline Group
LONDON
Distributed in the United States of America by
Oxford University Press Inc., New York

First published in Great Britain in 2004 by
Arnold, a member of the Hodder Headline Group,
338 Euston Road, London NW1 3BH

http://www.arnoldpublishers.com

Distributed in the United States of America by
Oxford University Press Inc.,
198 Madison Avenue, New York, NY 10016

The advice and information in this book are believed to be true and
accurate at the date of going to press, but neither the author nor the publisher
can accept any legal responsibility or liability for any errors or omissions.

British Library Cataloguing in Publication Data
A catalogue record for this book is available from the British Library

Library of Congress Cataloging-in-Publication Data
A catalog record for this book is available from the Library of Congress

ISBN 0 340 76325 6

1 2 3 4 5 6 7 8 9 10

Typeset in 10 on 13pt Sabon by Phoenix Photosetting, Chatham, Kent
Printed and bound in Malta

What do you think about this book? Or any other Arnold title?
Please send your comments to feedback.arnold@hodder.co.uk

Contents

Series editor's preface

The plural in the title of this series, *Contexts*, is intentional. Literature, while it emerges from, and responds to, historical, social, and cultural moments, also to a large extent establishes its own contexts, through the particular inflection it puts upon its ostensible 'materials', themes, and preoccupations. Therefore, rather than offering a traditional 'major works/historical background' parallel discussion, each *Contexts* volume takes its instigation from the ways in which literary texts have defined their areas of reference, and in which they are in active dialogue with key cultural ideas and events of their time. What aspects of a period most concerned writers? What effect upon literary form have various social and cultural trends had? How have different texts responded to single historical events? How do different texts, ultimately, 'speak back' to their period?

Historical background is made readily available in each volume, but is always closely integrated within discussion of literary texts. As such, the narrative woven around each literary historical period in the individual volumes follows no uniform pattern, but reflects their particular authors' sense of the ways in which the contexts of their period establish themselves – generically, thematically, or involving debates about language, gender, religion, or social change, for example. While each volume provides detailed discussion of its period's most studied literary works, it also asks informed questions about the canon and periodization itself. Each volume also contains a timeline, full bibliography, and several contemporary literary, cultural, or historical documents which provide material for further reflection and discussion.

Steven Matthews

Acknowledgements

I am grateful to the Modernist Journals Project at Brown University for permission to use an extract from the C. Grant Robertson article in *The New Age*. This book has benefited from many conversations with friends and colleagues over the years: Nathalie Blondel, Shirley Chew, Ian Fairley, Nancy Gish, Alex Goody, Sèan Hand, Hugh Haughton, Edward Larrissy, Alan Marshall, Nigel Messenger, Michael O'Neill, Catherine Morley, Stan Smith, Alistair Stead, Ashley Taggart, John Whale. My greatest debt, as ever, is to Elleke Boehmer, for her insightful and challenging reading of the book in manuscript, and for the delight she brings to the days. This book is for the lovely boys, Thomas and Sam.

1

Modernism: origins and overview

Prelude

In her episodic late novel *The Years* (1937), Virginia Woolf maps the history of a family from 1880 through to 'the present day', which internal textual evidence dates to around 1931–3. The changing lives of the Pargiters across this fifty-year period allow Woolf to explore many issues that will recur across this book exploring the contexts of modernism. Members of the family involve themselves, for instance, in several of the key political issues of the era, including the debates over Home Rule in Ireland and the fight for women's suffrage, which will figure in several discussions later in the book. The lead-in to the First World War, and a sense of the war's impact upon the civilian population of London from 1914 to 1918, is given prominence by Woolf as a moment which signalled the ending of one form of thought, culture, and civilization, and the beginning of another. Like the novel, this book subscribes, therefore, to an almost mythic reading of the historical trauma of the era, which is vital for much of modernism's self-definition, as we shall see.

The Years also situates itself within one of the dominating historical paradigms of the transition from the nineteenth to the twentieth century, a paradigm which signals something of the cultural and political uncertainty which underlies the modernist movement in literature. Several generations of the men in the novel become involved in the administration of the British Empire, and Woolf explores the impact of the imperial adventure upon its capital, London, through the varying effects that their experience of India and Africa has on the lives of this middle-class family. Colonel Pargiter, the head of the family at the start of the book, has lost two fingers from his right hand helping to suppress the so-called Indian Mutiny or Revolt (1857–8), a source of fascination and horror to his children. His son, Martin, is part of the colonial service in India and Africa, and remains an outsider upon his return to England, burying his feelings and unable to connect in relationships. Martin's cousin, North, returns in the 'present-day' section from farming in Africa, and offers a similar outsider's commentary upon what the family has become. By the end of the novel also, the independently minded Eleanor, Martin's sister, has travelled to India – even though she is over seventy – suggesting that, with the fading of the original Victorian imperial ambition, it is now women who seek the new perspectives offered by colonized territories.

Woolf's intimation through the engagement of each of these characters with the empire is that the very fabric of London, its streets and buildings as well as its people, comes to seem different when perceived through the lens of the imperial possessions. On reading a letter from Martin in 1891 about his having become lost overnight in the Indian jungle, Eleanor, riding in a taxi through central London, 'saw nothing but stunted little trees, and her brother looking at the sun rising over the jungle. The sun was rising. Flames for a moment danced over the vast funereal mass of the Law Courts.'[1] The centre of British imperial justice seems threatened by, and deadly beneath, the actual experience of lostness and fear imbued by the attempt to instil such 'civilizing' virtues across the globe. As the black American activist and organizer of the first pan-African congress seeking liberty for enslaved nations (which took place in London in 1900), W. E. B. Dubois, had noted a decade earlier than Woolf's novel: 'with nearly every great European empire to-day walks its dark colonialist shadow'.[2]

It is with the meditations of North, newly returned from Africa, at a party in the concluding 'present-day' section of *The Years*, however, that the major shift of emphasis Woolf perceives to have taken place across this historical period becomes realized. Early parts of the novel had emphasized the domestic rituals and sociability (the tea table), and the communal political action (suffragism, voluntary help for the poor), which characterized late Victorian life and held its middle-class families together. North now reflects that such communal centring of lives has taken on a threatening possibility in the 1930s, with the advent of Fascism ('hot halls and reverberating microphones . . . black shirts, green shirts, red shirts'). But he also suggests that, contrary to earlier communal phases of nineteenth-century living, it is now the individual who has become the focus of what meaning there is to be made of 'the present'. Everyone has, in the 1930s, 'to begin inwardly, and let the devil take the outer form' (p. 300). In Woolf's reading of historical transition across the years 1880–1930, as in the reading of many of the other writers featured in this book, the essential change is from an externally ratified and public mode of understanding to a personal and individual one.

It is a transition from dependence upon social and progressive forms of living to a more ambiguous and complex sense of *interiority* within the individual who is seeking to 'make sense' of the contemporary world.

Characteristically, here as in other modernist works, North's self-doubt has gone so far as to lead him to question his own ability to make meaning at all: 'But what do I mean, he wondered . . .?' In the wake of the First World War, everything has come to seem less certain: 'a little blur had come round the edges of things . . . Things seemed to have lost their skins; to be freed from some surface hardness' (p. 210). North's meditations, therefore, both reflect this historical obscuring, and suggest that, with the new emphasis upon individuality over the collective, meaning itself becomes harder to fix and sustain.

The trajectory plotted across Woolf's *The Years* is, then, one from a settled Victorian world and sense of 'civilized' and 'civilizing' values to an unstable modern one; from an imperial world, towards a post-imperial one; from a world in which gender relations seemed founded upon set inequality (woman commanding domestic space as an Angel of the House, man as public upholder of national values) to one in which women are equally if not *more* purposively and politically active than men. It is a move from a sense of collective purpose to a world of individual scepticism and self-doubt. Woolf several times alludes in the latter pages of her novel to the turn-of-the-century novel *Heart of Darkness* (1899) by Joseph Conrad. In the first of these echoes of Conrad's title, Eleanor reflects upon the vast city of London beyond the privileged circle of her middle-class milieu, a world 'indifferent to this world, of people toiling, grinding, in the heart of darkness, in the depths of night' (p. 284).

The second reference is closer to Conrad's original context, as North reflects upon his African experience and turns it into a metaphysical version of his own struggle to make sense of the world: 'He felt that he had been in the middle of the jungle; in the heart of darkness; cutting his way towards the light; but provided only with broken sentences, single words' (p. 301). Woolf's allusions in her book to Conrad's original mean that the anonymous hellishness of London, the contemporary centre of civilization, is mirrored in the inadequacy with which the character confronts 'uncivilized' realities. In the process, 'civilization' itself comes into question. Terms like 'external' and 'internal' become themselves irrelevant in describing these experiences, since what had hitherto seemed the 'external' world (London) has become haunted both by the uncertain outcomes of the imperial adventure and by a sense of its own meaninglessness. It is a sense of meaninglessness matched in the minds of the most percipient of the characters in the novel.

The Years traces these issues to their origin in late Victorian life, where a time of empty social ritual moves towards one in which a new sensibility begins to form itself. But it is an uneven and uncertain movement, one in which no one character in the book comes to dominate or direct our sense of what the book might be taken to mean. At the end, like North, we are left with a sense of the inadequacy of former modes of expression to register the extreme experiences of the age, but unclear as to the nature of new and better ways of characterizing and expressing them.

Thematically, most of the texts that will be considered in this study share many of the historical, cultural, and philosophical recognitions of *The Years*. This holds not just for those texts written by English writers, but also by those British, Irish, and American novelists, dramatists, and poets who arrived in London in the latter part of the nineteenth century and in the early years of the twentieth, preceding the 1914 outbreak of world war.[3] Issues of value, questions about civilization, gender relations, imperial destiny, and religion resonate through many texts of this period. London was, at the time, centre to the largest empire on the planet, and, as Jonathan Schneer has argued, 'it was impossible, in turn-of-the-century London, to avoid the imperial subtext'. As part of the urbanization which took place in many parts of Britain in the later years of the nineteenth century (an urbanization which was to have its own effects on the evolution of a distinctively modern consciousness, as we shall see), London's population had nearly doubled. By 1911, it had reached nearly seven and a quarter million.[4] The architectural massiveness of the buildings of imperial government, the vast Port of London bringing goods from across the empire into the country, the ostentatious wealth generated in the City's financial houses, and the various forms of popular entertainment, from Regent's Park Zoo to imperial shows and exhibitions, all underlined the city's status.[5] As such, the city was both the political and the cultural capital of the empire.

But London also drew in people active in both cultural and political spheres, as Schneer shows, who resisted the imperial values upon which the city was currently founded. It provided a magnet for those of advanced political views, including feminism and socialism, as never before. Those seeking freedom from family ties and sheltered provincial ideas from England and across the English-speaking world flocked to the city in the 1890s and early 1900s. At the same time, the capital was unavoidable for those with literary ambition, and this was to provide an important example and impetus for early modernism, as this book will reveal.[6]

Amongst the Americans, the novelist Henry James pioneered the way by moving to London in 1876. The poet Ezra Pound arrived in 1908 and was followed by his fellow poet Hilda Doolittle (know by her initials H. D.) in 1911. T. S. Eliot arrived in the summer of 1914, just before the outbreak of war. From the Anglo-Irish, George Bernard Shaw had arrived in 1876; Oscar Wilde was there from the early 1880s; W. B. Yeats had spent much of his time, following a childhood move to Fitzroy Road in 1867, between London and rural Ireland. The young James Joyce briefly entertained the possibility of working in London, before escaping to Paris, the city which formed an alternative centre for Anglophone modernism (particularly for Americans), with renewed impetus in the years following World War One. Other writers from the empire (Ireland did not obtain independence, and then only partially so, until 1922) were similarly drawn by the possibilities offered by the capital. The South African Olive Schreiner had been fêted for her novel *The Story of an African Farm* (1883) during a brief stay in England; she settled there twenty years later and became an important commentator upon a range of political and women's issues. The important story writer exploring new possibilities for women's lives, the Australian George Egerton (Mary Chavelita Bright), settled in London in the 1890s after her travels, and was lionized by Shaw and Yeats amongst others. The short-story writer Katherine Mansfield arrived from New Zealand in London to complete her education and, after 1908, never returned to her native country. The Polish émigré Conrad settled in England after his marriage in 1896.

London also proved the inevitable destination for British writers connected with the origins and development of modernism, writers often seeking to escape the personal and literary limitations of a regional upbringing. The Yorkshire-born novelist George Gissing lived with an ex-prostitute, Nell Harrison, in London from 1877. H. G. Wells arrived from Kent to study in 1884. The poet and critic Arthur Symons, who, as we shall shortly see, crucially mediated current French poetic thinking to poets writing in English in the 1890s, had arrived from a limiting low-church Cornish upbringing. Later, D. H. Lawrence was a schoolmaster in Croydon in 1908–11, during the formative years of his ambitions as a prose writer, and met key figures like Pound, Yeats, and Ford Madox Ford. Later still, the novelist Mary Butts arrived from Dorset to study at various London colleges and stayed, working for London County Council, during the First World War. Other writers key to modernism, including Woolf, Charlotte Mew, E. M. Forster, and Wyndham Lewis were, of course, familiar with the city from childhood.

This listing is not to deny the significance of alternative centres for modernism in Paris or, slightly later, in New York. Joyce was in Paris from the early 1900s and found the publisher for his scandalous text, *Ulysses,* there rather than in England. The American prose writer Gertrude Stein was in Paris from 1903. Pound resettled there in late 1920, drawn by the more vibrant post-war artistic and cultural life, and Ernest Hemingway soon joined him. F. Scott and Zelda Fitzgerald often passed through; the Dominican-born Jean Rhys moved from London and was to be based in Paris during the early years of her writing career. For all of these writers, Paris represented an escape from the constraining social, cultural, and personal atmosphere of their childhood. The city also offered freedom from the intellectual provincialism in which they were raised; personally, it offered possibilities for sexual freedom, including the enjoyment of same-sex relations which were crucial for the establishment of 'alternative modernisms', as Shari Benstock as argued. Particularly for lesbian American women writers, including Stein, H. D., Djuna Barnes, Sylvia Beach (publisher of Joyce's *Ulysses*), and (after 1921) the editors of the crucial modernist magazine *Little Review,* Jane Heap and Margaret Anderson, Paris provided open-minded coteries in which there was support, context, and an audience for their work.[7]

My focus upon the London context in this chapter about the beginnings of modernism is not blind, I should emphasize, to the different but related emergence of a modernist sensibility amongst American authors who resisted a move to Europe. These writers sought to found their sense of modern literature upon a native grain of voice and attitude. They included Marianne Moore, William Carlos Williams, Wallace Stevens, and, later, William Faulkner. The United States had, from 1880 onwards, seen a period of rapid urbanization on a par with that experienced in Britain. It was an urbaniza-tion that was accompanied by a colossal growth in the industrial base of the country – there was a nine-fold increase in capital invested in manufacturing across this period. By the time of the First World War in 1914, the urban population exceeded the rural, and the ten largest cities of America, includ-ing New York, Chicago, Philadelphia, and Boston, had experienced a three-fold growth from the later years of the nineteenth century.[8] Writers on the other side of the Atlantic were, simultaneously, experiencing similar kinds of alienation and social uncertainty to those that I have been discussing in connection with *The Years*. I will review the impact of these developments in later chapters. The unequalled phenomenon of literary expatriation from America, as mentioned in the cases of Pound, Eliot, Stein, Fitzgerald, and Hemingway, is again a marker of this uncertainty. The emphasis of this opening chapter, however, will be upon the literary developments in London created by the native British and international émigré nexus of figures from the 1890s to the early 1910s. It was a nexus which in poetry, drama, and the novel established the distinctive features of what has subsequently become recognized as Anglo-American modernist literature.

When and what was modernism?

Before discussing these developments, however, it is perhaps necessary to ask a more fundamental question about the nature of this as a distinctive literary period. Many works to be discussed in this chapter and later in the book position themselves, as I have said earlier, in relation to a similar sense of the period's trajectory to that outlined in Woolf's *The Years*. But does that mean that the response of these various authors in various genres to the issues raised by the period 1890–1930 share enough common ground to denominate the period *modernist*? The writers mentioned above, after all, embrace a variety of literary modes and styles, often radically different from each other – modes and styles often also related to the writers' sense of distinctive national literary inheritances. *Thematically* and perceptually there is much convergence between these writers, but in terms of their modes of deploying their writing in literary form, they are markedly diverse. What, then, distinguishes and defines such writing as *modernist*?

Literary historians have resolved this dilemma about 'modernist' styles according to a range of preferences and sometimes in quite radical ways. Some commentators, including key American critics like Charles Altieri and Marjorie Perloff, have established a split between those writers who are most interested in contesting traditional modes of literary representation and others who, despite views politically or literarily anti-traditional, do not experiment formally. In this mode of literary history, Ezra Pound, Gertrude Stein, and James Joyce, all of whom sought to break away from previous forms of representation in their various genres, would join the Italian Futurist poet and manifesto-maker Filippo Marinetti and the French Surrealists to form a European avant-garde. Avant-garde experimentalism then becomes the favoured term to denote the most exciting literature, music, and painting of the period, its radical newness. Other literary historians, including most recently Peter Nicholls in his survey *Modernisms*, have sought a more inclusive approach to the literature of the time: one that embraces Futurism and Surrealism whilst at the same time not inhibiting discussion of the achievements of such writers as D. H. Lawrence and Woolf.

Several recent critics have also questioned a tension within readings of British-based modernism which had become something of a critical commonplace. This is a tension between identification of that writing which might be typically labelled 'modernist', and that which might be seen under the more conservative banner as 'Edwardian' (after the king at the time), a tension 'with the attendant privileging of modernist over Edwardian'. Rather, it is suggested by Carola M. Kaplan and Anne B. Simpson, there are 'interpenetrations and intersections' between modernist and Edwardian literature. Many 'modernist' writers, including D. H. Lawrence, E. M. Forster, and Virginia Woolf, display traits bridging the native and traditional, and the aggressively international literary possibilities, at the time.[9] Yet again, an innovative recent collection of essays edited by Lynne Hapgood and Nancy L. Paxton has sought to overturn the boundaries sustained by earlier critics. These are boundaries between a reading of modernism as an inveterately avant-garde and experimental ideal, and the kinds of critical realism that held sway in the nineteenth-century British social novel. Rather, Hapgood and Paxton argue, they understand 'realism and modernism as terms which describe literary techniques rather than define conflictual literary movements'. These techniques are then taken uniquely to interact and often to co-exist within the same text at this period.[10] It is this technical interaction between realism and modernism that I shall pursue throughout this book, as it impacts upon the perceptual and material qualities of texts during the period.

'Modernism' is, of course, anyway a term applied to the literary writing of this period *retrospectively*. The historical resonance of the word 'modernism' as a counter to play when describing uniform aspects of the period, however, reveals many of the tensions which would be expanded upon in subsequent critical responses to its texts. The *Oxford English Dictionary* cites 'modernism' as having arisen in the Battle of the Books between the ancients and the moderns – the favourers of literary models provided by the past and those who drew inspiration from contemporary trends – in the early eighteenth century. The negative charge of the early usage for the term is apparent in the main *OED* definition: 'A usage, mode of expression, or peculiarity of style or workmanship, characteristic of modern times.' Note the ambivalence of that 'peculiarity', which is more than sustained by the initial citation supporting the definition, which comes from an epistle from Jonathan Swift to Alexander Pope in 1737, railing at 'Scribblers . . . who send us over their trash in Prose and Verse, with abominable curtailings and quaint modernisms'. Only in 1830 does the dictionary suggest that 'modernism' took on a more neutral definition of 'sympathy with or affinity to what is modern'.

That tension between past and present, which is a tension about individual value and sympathy as much as one about ideology, is played out in the subsequent history of the term 'modernism', not least, as has been suggested above, in critical readings of the historical period covered by this book. It is a tension present in an important example from early in the 1890s. As her ideal lover, Angel Clare, courts her, Tess of the D'Urbervilles in Hardy's novel of that title becomes depressed that her love for him is doomed to tragic failure. Angel is ignorant of the fact that she has had a baby by another man. Out of her depression at his probable rejection of her once he knows her secret come some melancholy reflections on the nature of existence which seem to Angel's ear extraordinary when uttered by one whom he takes to be a simple milkmaid of limited experience and expectations:

> She was expressing in her own native phrases – assisted a little by her Sixth Standard training – feelings which might be called those of the age – the ache of modernism. The perception arrested him less when he reflected that what are called advanced ideas are really but the latest fashion in definition.[11]

Angel's acceptance of a definition of 'modernism' as simply 'the latest fashion', 'contemporaneity', marks his own weakness and his inability to understand Tess's situation, which leads to the farcical failure of their marriage. Just a few pages earlier than this passage, Hardy has alerted us to the fact that Angel had been ignorantly accepting of fashionable ideas until he arrived at the farm where he met Tess. It was there and then that he freed himself of that 'chronic melancholy which is taking hold of the civilized races with the decline of belief in a beneficent Power' (p. 118). Hardy's sense is, rather, that Tess's 'ache of modernism' has partly arisen in her because of advances in women's education after the 1870 Education Act, which made education compulsory and which gradually raised the school-leaving age to fourteen. (The Act brought advances, particularly for women, which resonate again and again across this book.) Tess's 'modernism' gives her a broader perspective upon her experiences and upon the direction the world is taking for good or ill than Clare can achieve.

From this point of view, Tess's 'modernism' seems confirmed by the very structuring of the novel named ironically for her, since, in its early edition, Tess's life was divided by Hardy into seven 'phases'. The word 'Phases' used for the sub-sections of the book suggests the transience of any one of Tess's states and stages of life, and also accounts for the breaks in narrative between the various parts of her story. In the break between the first 'phase', 'The Maiden', and the second, 'Maiden No More', which narrates events following her forced encounter with Alec D'Urberville, Tess herself has become 'somewhat changed – the same, but not the same', as we are told (p. 89). We are reminded here, as elsewhere in the novel, though, that Tess's 'changes' are not something she is in control of, but are forced upon this 'pure woman' (as the novel's sub-title controversially asserted her to be) through her appalling treatment by the males she encounters, including Clare. Tess's 'modernism' marks her victimhood as much as it is an understanding of it. The implications of this reading, both positive and negative, in terms of the relation of 'modernism' to women's situation in contemporary society, will be pursued across this book.

Similar tensions and ambiguities about implied values and judgements to these in Hardy exist in the prevalence of the term 'modernism' between the later 1890s and the late 1920s. Indeed, 'modernism' was used in the period of our concern not as a word to be applied to literature at all, but rather as one within the dominant *theological* debates of the time. Modernist theologians were anxious to establish the symbolic (rather than the historical or scientific) meaning of biblical testimony. They asserted the interconnection between sacred and profane spheres, and resisted modern scientific attacks upon evidences for faith, as is indicated by a book like Alfred Fawkes's *Modernism*, which appeared in a whole series called *Studies in Modernism* in 1913. Essays by clerics calling themselves 'modernists' were appearing in little magazines like *The New Age* at the same time as innovative literary works from authors such as Pound or Katherine Mansfield.

It is, then, a leap from the definition of 'modernism' current at the time such literary writers were working to that which has achieved currency within more recent university degree courses. Stan Smith has done very helpful work in establishing the origins of the term 'modernism' as a critical tool both outside and within the academy. In a letter to the *London Review of Books* of 7 June 2001, Smith notes that the term was originally used in the early 1920s by critics from the American south, including John Crowe Ransom and Allen Tate. For them, the term denominated the kind of poetry then being written by T. S. Eliot and Ezra Pound. 'Modernism' got surprisingly translated into Britain in 1927 through the title of Robert Graves' and Laura Riding's study of contemporary work: *A Survey of Modernist Poetry*.[12] The term was not, however, applied by Graves and Riding positively to the Poundian mode, of which they were often critical, but rather to the emerging strain of *English* poetry from W. H. Auden and his associates. The term 'modernism' entered universities via this route, and also in the United States via the generation of critic-poets after Tate and Ransom.

Even from this genealogy, however, it is clear that the meaning of 'modernism' is for some time highly unsettled, whilst also being one related to genre-specific, poetic, issues. In America it is related very much to the ideas taken to be integral to Pound and Eliot's work, as signalled, for instance, by a 1939 book by Cleanth Brooks, another critic in the group around Allen Tate and John Crowe Ransom: *Modern Poetry and the Tradition*. The past history of any poetic form is taken by Brooks to form a kind of ordering organic system in which each modern poem can be interrelated to past poems. Each new poem (and Brooks's ideas directly reflect Eliot's in essays like his 1919 'Tradition and the Individual Talent' in this) then offers its own distinctive formal unity which carries the tradition further forward. It is possible to detect – and this is the critic's task of 'understanding' – within each poem a pattern of issues and oppositions which it is the triumph of the poetic form to bring to a harmonic resolution and aesthetically satisfying conclusion.

Paradoxically, therefore, for Brooks, as for others of the so-called New Critics in his circle, 'modernism' offers a conservative and even reactionary literary and social possibility. Poetry is seen to present a continuing model of order and wholeness which proves exemplary within an increasingly technologized, chaotic, and fragmented modern world. There is an obvious recourse to tradition visible on the surfaces of the poetry of Pound and Eliot, in their persistent allusiveness to earlier texts and deployment of often recondite historical subject matter. But this recourse is perceived by Brooks to be in fact a marker of a continuity existent between former and current ways of perceiving and being in the world. New Criticism offers, as we shall see, a contentious reading of the actual processes active in the work of Pound and Eliot, as in that of other 'modernist' writers. But it also tells us much about the political and academic interests invested in the description of the new writing emerging in the early part of the twentieth century as 'modernist'.

Conversely and confusingly, as Smith demonstrates, in Britain the term was applied to what we might now think of as the generation of writers emerging *after* the high 'modernist' moment had passed. The poets of the 1930s grouped around W. H. Auden would seem to have at least partly resisted the procedures of Eliot in particular, writing a difficult poetry, yes, but one without the immediate literary self-reference of works like Eliot's *The Waste Land*. Auden in particular seems anxious to return *English* poetry to its origins in Anglo-Saxon alliterative verse. The siting of much of his 'modernist' early work is away from the metropolis of London so favoured by early Eliot and Pound, in the mining and Pennine landscape familiar to him from his childhood. In this company, the view of 'modernism' as an 'international' phenomenon, which has continued in criticism from both America and England down to the present, seems again to be questionable. The inheritance of the term as descriptive of a specific literary period in British universities can seem an unknowing translation of American academic presumptions, to the neglect of more specific and local English, and more broadly British, innovation and realignments within the tradition.

These splits and splittings within the origins of the term itself also demonstrate an uncertainty over the dating of the so-called 'modernist' period. The New Critical assumption would seem to limit the reference of the term to work emerging in the 1910s and continuing through to, perhaps, the Second World War (taking the publication date of Brooks's *Modern Poetry and the Tradition* as emblematic). The original British perspective suggests rather that modernism is a phenomenon of the 1930s. And yet it might be queried whether the 'modernist' moment has even now passed. The breezily applied term 'postmodern', such a standby in contemporary criticism of all the arts, would suggest a post-1945 rejection of many of the earlier twentieth-century formal and textual presumptions. Yet recent criticism of modernist authors, criticism itself informed by recent theoretical and philosophical insights, has suggested that the work of, say, Ezra Pound demonstrates many of the radical uncertainties over economies of meaning which are now taken as the currency of *post*modern writing.[13] For all the claims made by critics to discover a struggle for 'coherence' and order within modernist texts, there remains a countering sense of a lack of finitude, organization, and 'meaning' in them. As the final chapter of this book argues, this countering sense challenges easy acceptance of the distinction between writing from the early half of the twentieth century and that of the later.

'And I am not a demigod. I cannot make it cohere', as Pound famously lamented in Canto CXVI, towards the end of the voyage represented by his epic poem *The Cantos*, which had taken over fifty years to assemble. This suggests a failure of the presumed divine power of authorship correlative to that of Roland Barthes in his notorious essay on 'The Death of the Author'. Barthes celebrates the birth of the text and the reader of the text over and above the meanings which the writer has striven to put there – this is an essay, therefore, in which inhere many of the strategies of 'postmodern' literary debate. And yet the reminder provided by Pound's *Cantos*, many of which are presented to us as 'Drafts and Fragments' and not as finally completed works, admonishes all complacent attempts at periodization in relation to the literary works of the twentieth century. It also admonishes any complacent sense that 'modernism' has somehow stopped as a set of identifiable literary devices or procedures.

Such complications in defining the term 'modernism' return us as students and readers to a necessary inquiry into the *actual* contexts and origins of each individual text. This is particularly so of those texts of the earlier part of the twentieth century now read as being emblematic in their engagement with shifts in understanding which went to initiate the modern world as we understand it. These texts are emblematic also in providing more recent writing from authors as diverse as Adrienne Rich and Don DeLillo in the United States to Geoffrey Hill and Jeanette Winterson in the UK, as well as postcolonial writers including Salman Rushdie and Derek Walcott, with a set of signposts or markers as to how that modern world might be registered on the page. This book will therefore everywhere pay attention to the literary, social, and national contexts arising from the texts themselves, rather than seeking to align them with an academic preconception as to their nature. It will consider the texts as a response to, and engagement with, concerns of the immediate present out of which they were written. This is a present which is always inflected by an author's personal and political interests, seeking to make a particular engagement with both the precise history of the times and with broader issues arising in the present from a reading of historical and literary-historical inheritance.

This book will consider a range of texts in so far as they raise specific locations within specific historical dynamics, rather than seeking to marshal them into intertextual, or 'movement'-based, relations to each other or to the times. The modernist 'canon' is frequently being added to, particularly through exciting research into hitherto neglected women writers of the period, such as Mary Butts, Mina Loy, May Sinclair, and Sylvia Townsend Warner.[14] This is research which is partly concerned to redress the earlier damaging critical concentration upon the major male figures of the period in books like Hugh Kenner's 1972 *The Pound Era*. Yet, in other senses, the 'canon' remains in place. The reputations of various key figures like Eliot, Woolf, and Lawrence have gone up and down, but they remain the representative figures of modernism for both students and within broader English-speaking culture. In this book, therefore, although I do introduce other voices, my concentration for constraints of space will be mainly upon these central figures. For the rest of this chapter, I will focus upon those social and cultural trends in the late part of the nineteenth century which continued and developed in the first twenty years of the twentieth, and pursue the literary ideas which arose within those contexts.

Individualism, literature, and private life

At issue for many political theorists, thinkers, and literary writers across the latter years of the nineteenth century and into the twentieth was the relation between the collective, or society, and the individual. With the rise of the new sociology in Europe, through such influential writers as Emile Durkheim and Max Weber, and more concertedly in the USA, debates about what held society together and about the tendency of society to disempower individuals became predominant. With the rise of socialism as a labour movement in Britain, and in the thinking (after 1884) of Fabian Socialists such as Beatrice and Sidney Webb, the (often negative) impact of the social structure on individual lives was scrutinized. The National Association for the Promotion of Social Science was founded in Britain in the 1870s, followed by the Sociological Society in the early 1900s. Such bodies established an atmosphere of intellectual inquiry in which issues of personal identity were weighed against class and gender relationships, national character, and the need for social change, particularly in the situation of women. What all of these trends across the world signified was a questioning (and in some cases a reassertion) of the status of the individual within a newly urbanized and increasingly industrialized society which was alienating and prejudicial to it.[15] Such questions received added impulse in the English-speaking world from the new science of such as Karl Pearson, whose 1892 *The Grammar of Science* concluded that the world is for us simply our 'sense-impressions', and from the developing realm of anthropology. Sir James G. Frazer's mammoth work *The Golden Bough* (first volume published in 1890), discussed more fully in Chapter 4 below, offered an evolutionary reading of human society which viewed it as founded upon ancient myth and ritual. Beneath every modern person, he claimed to have discovered a primitive set of desires and ideals which reconfigured for the age its sense of culture, society, and the individual.

The ideas underlying the rhetoric of literary radicalism just before the First World War, and into the early 1920s, continued to reflect upon these issues, principally in their meditation upon the issue of the significance (or otherwise) of personality, individual consciousness, and experience. In this there is continuity in many aspects of mid- to late nineteenth-century ideas in Britain and America and the preoccupations of the modernists.[16] In America from the late 1880s, the Harvard philosopher William James was considering the relation between biological and environmental circumstance and everyday life, and personal choice and belief, concluding that individual consciousness was the site of all understanding and ideas. From the mid-nineteenth century, English writers such as Matthew Arnold and, perhaps more tellingly in this instance, Walter Pater, were moving towards new conceptions of the relation between the individual and history, the individual and cultural traditions, the individual and society. These ideas in their turn would provide examples for key figures like Pound, Eliot, Joyce, and Woolf in the early part of the next century. The iconic moment here would be Pater's notorious Conclusion to his collection of essays *The Renaissance* (1873), a conclusion that proved so scandalous that Pater himself suppressed it for the work's second and third editions:

> At first sight experience seems to bury us under a flood of external objects . . . But when reflexion begins to play upon those objects they

are dissipated under its influence . . . each object is loosed into a group of impressions – colour, odour, texture – in the mind of the observer . . . Experience, already reduced to a group of impressions, is ringed around for each one of us by that thick wall of personality through which no real voice has ever pierced on its way to us, or from us to that which we can only conjecture to be without . . . Not the fruit of experience, but experience itself, is the end . . . To burn always with this hard, gem-like flame, to maintain this ecstasy, is success in life. In a sense it might even be said that our failure is to form habits.[17]

Pater's elegantly crafted sentences offer an attack upon many of the habitual assurances which had sustained the early parts of the Victorian period. They signal that shift from a location of experience in an exterior world ('a flood of external objects') to that of an interior consciousness bounded by a 'thick world of personality' which I have discussed above as the dominant transition made across the modernist period. For Pater, notions of public service, of progress in scientific and technological realms, of domestic duty and religious observance, of the civilizing mission of imperialism – all are put into doubt by the reversion to the individual and individualism which is made here.

Rather than being able to sustain a controlled perspective upon the world, Pater's vision is that we are all initially overwhelmed by it. Our minds seek to sort amongst the welter of perceived 'external objects', but can only create 'impressions' of what the world offers us, not sustained and coherent 'meanings', religious or otherwise. There is no longer even a consensus view of what the world is, since we are all prisoners locked into our individual consciousness, and are neither susceptible to other 'voices' nor able to influence others in our turn. The danger in Pater's vision is that he concludes that we must accept this individualism as our fate, live in the moment, and make decisions based upon impulse, not received ethics. We lapse into solipsism and live accordingly. It is this kind of thinking which was labelled 'decadence', and, in the realm of the arts, was taken to mean that art's traditional moral duty no longer held true. The cult of self-regarding, 'art for art's sake' creativity was born.

In other words, as the final sentences quoted from Pater above imply, we must all seize the moment, the 'ecstasy' of passing experiences, regardless of admonishments from any moral or ethical system external to ourselves. The past and history, in so far as they may be said to exist, are performed in the individual's experience of the present; they do not exist as separate ideas which can be studied in isolation from present 'impressions'. Pater's vision, in other words, partakes of that tension which in historians' eyes is manifested right across the period 1870–1914 in Britain. This is a tension between the forces of a modern urban and industrial life which imposed greater conformity upon the population, whilst also contradictorily generating a new set of values to put upon private experience, and the importance of individual tastes and beliefs.[18]

The further impact of Pater's thought, as it manifested itself across the 1890s, was the implicit suggestion that art and literature should relinquish their 'improving' and 'educative' moral purpose – a purpose which had existed earlier in the nineteenth century through, for instance, William Wordsworth's example to Victorian novelists. Rather, for Pater, art assumes the nature of that impressionism which we all share in our responses to the world. In the last decade of the nineteenth century, this notion became inextricably tied to the emergence of a movement (often modelled upon French originals) towards literary and personal decadence. The most notorious of Pater's disciples in this regard was the Anglo-Irishman Oscar Wilde, whose plays, including *Lady Windermere's Fan, An Ideal Husband,* and *The Importance of Being Earnest* (all produced in London between 1892 and 1895), satirized the predominant habits and mores of the English middle classes. Wilde's only novel, *The Picture of Dorian Gray* (1891), offers an exploration of the Paterian countervailing ideal of individualism, decadence, and art for art's sake. This is principally achieved through its central conceit, in which Gray as it were changes places with his painted portrait, so that he remains ageless whilst the figure in the picture moves towards its death.

From the outset of the novel, Gray is cast as Personality incarnate, as is evident in the view of him given after his first, homoerotic, encounter with Basil Hallward, painter of the portrait: 'A curious sensation of terror came over me. I knew that I had come face to face with some one whose mere personality was so fascinating that, if I allowed it to do so, it would absorb my whole nature, my whole soul, my very art itself.'[19] Having cheated death by as it were changing places with the figure in his portrait, Gray relishes a life of luxury, sensuality, and decadence. He burns with 'a hard gem-like flame', to adopt Pater's view of 'success in life'. That indulgence serves to further for him the vision of the self he has favoured from the outset (p. 137):

> He used to wonder at the shallow psychology of those who conceive the Ego in man as a thing simple, permanent, reliable, and of one essence. To him, man was a being with myriad lives and myriad sensations, a complex multiform creature that bore within itself strange legacies of thought and passion, and whose very flesh was tainted with the monstrous maladies of the dead.

Gray's version of the Ego as a quality subject to present impressions over stable truths is what draws him to love an impoverished actress, Sibyl Vane, yet she, ironically, as the true performer, relishes the possibility of 'reality' and constancy which Gray's love offers. As a result of this clash of perspectives the lovers part. The scenes of the lovers' disagreement and their aftermath seem to take us to the centre of the novel's ambiguities around its central conceit. Gray, for whom 'Life itself was the first, the greatest, of the arts' (p. 125), is finally a tragic figure, one unable to find fulfilment in the only realm available to him. He becomes, paradoxically, the supreme artist, but only by becoming (a recognition of the solipsistic danger of Paterian thought) detached from the rest of reality (p. 138):

> There were times when it appeared to Dorian Gray that the whole of history was merely the record of his own life, not as he had lived it in act and circumstance, but as his imagination had created it for him.

By the end of the novel, Gray is no longer able to sustain that isolation, and commits suicide. Wilde's exploration of the lived decadent life proves, then, an unsettling one. Many of the Paterian concerns which will manifest themselves in modernism – the variousness of the Ego, the importance of art over life in a world of religious and social uncertainty – are qualified in Gray's fall from love and interest in Life.

Declan Kiberd, viewing Wilde as a figure in the literature of a still-colonized Ireland, has seen that very ambiguity as the virtue of Wilde's pose with regard to the English social and literary mainstream. Gray shares Wilde's personal delight in performance (in 'myriad lives and myriad sensations') in the novel. Gray's correlative disbelief in the value of sincerity and consistency were Wilde's also. The mainstays of English late Victorian self-importance are therefore being implicitly satirized.[20] And yet the final scene of the novel is also darker than this implies. In Gray's gruesome end, Wilde questions the sustainability of decadent hedonism as a perspective upon the world. He asks whether the individual, however isolated and indulgent, is finally victim to 'strange legacies of thought and passion', and the almost physical tainting of the past. The delight in performance here is marked also by a sense of fatal haunting by the past from which the individual is not finally free. Such haunting will recur across later modernist literature, in, say, the drifting fragmentary voices of T. S. Eliot's *The Waste Land*.[21]

Wilde's personal pursuit of 'decadence', of course, brought him to the trials in which he was convicted of sodomy in 1895, trials which rapidly assumed iconic significance in the debates about individualism and the social order in the later part of the decade. Wilde's homosexuality, coded in the relation between Lord Henry Wotton and Gray in his novel, allied decadence to sexual adventurousness. In its turn, Wilde's public disgrace, as Sally Ledger has argued, brought to an end a time when an overt challenge to Victorian sexual codes was being offered from various quarters. 'Decadence' was a term applied with relish by socially conservative critics to the so-called New Women novelists, whose openness about women's sexuality had overturned standard nineteenth-century narrative practices centred upon marriage plots.[22] One of the New Women writers, George Egerton, for instance, claimed that for women 'There was only one small plot left for her to tell: the *terra incognita* of herself, as she knew herself to be, not as man liked to imagine her.'[23] That unknown territory at the time, a woman's thoughts, feelings, and desires, would become a key impetus to modernist exploration and experimentation by both male and female writers in the 1910s.

As Extract 1 printed on p. 140 makes clear – it comes from May Sinclair's famous 1918 article on her fellow woman novelist Dorothy Richardson – the issue of gender is intimately allied in modernist writing with that of literary experimentation (although Sinclair herself does not make it such). More specifically, Sinclair's reflections seem to offer a culminating solution (and an influential one for writers like Virginia Woolf) within the debates which we have contemplated in this section of the opening chapter. The definitive issue of how realistically to render individual consciousness in the modern world finds itself distilled by Sinclair as a question of how to put onto the page the 'stream of consciousness' of an ordinary woman in her everyday life (she takes this phrase from William James). In the process, expectations about the formal ordering and structuring of the novel (its beginning, middle, and end) come into question, as also does the writer's hitherto authoritative position with regard to the material of the text. With the new view of the individual developed across these years through new academic interests such as sociology (and soon psychology) and contemporary political debate, the question of individualism and literary form undertook different configurations to any accepted earlier. These new views in their turn instigated several of the ambitions and formulations of modernism itself.

Symbolism, Imagism, and drama

An inheritance from Paterian individualism, which had a significant impact upon the development of literary ideas in what we now think of as modernism, was provided by a further link between the literary innovation of the 1890s and the radical literary communities of the 1910s. The Cornish critic and poet, Arthur Symons, saw Pater as the most important influence upon his early thought, culminating in his 1899 study *The Symbolist Movement in Literature*.[24] *The Symbolist Movement* became a key text in the development of many early twentieth-century authors, and particularly of poets. The Anglo-Irish poet W. B. Yeats, Symons's erstwhile friend and flat-mate, and the dedicatee of *The Symbolist Movement*, responded with his major essay declaring the method of his own work, the 1900 'The Symbolism of Poetry'. In his 1920 essay 'The Perfect Critic', T. S. Eliot described the experience of reading Symons's book (which he did in December 1908) as 'an introduction to wholly new feelings ... a revelation'.[25] In a letter of as late as 1928, Ezra Pound, too, acknowledged the significance of the nexus of Symbolists which included Yeats, Symons, the French poet Stéphane Mallarmé, and the English philosopher T.E. Hulme as underlying his own literary-propagandist project, Imagism, which will shortly be discussed.[26]

In *The Symbolist Movement in Literature,* Symons brought the influence of Pater, and his love for the dramatic monologues of Robert Browning (a poet who would prove important also to Pound), to bear upon his reading of recent French poetry. The book contains chapters on a group of poets loosely grouped as the 'Symbolists' – Gérard de Nerval, Villiers de L'Isle-Adam, Arthur Rimbaud, Paul Verlaine, Jules Laforgue (who was to prove the main excitement in the book for Eliot when he first read it, and to influence many of his early works), Stéphane Mallarmé, Maurice Maeterlinck, and J.-L. Huysmans (whose sacred book *A Rebours* lay behind Wilde's decadence in *The Picture of Dorian Gray*). Symons's description of this group of poets resonates with a sense of their experimental difference from mid-nineteenth-century French poetry and finds many echoes in the criticism later aimed at poetry in English, including work by Pound and Eliot, as they sought to define their modern distinctiveness:

> [Symbolism] is all an attempt to spiritualise literature, to evade the old bondage of rhetoric, the old bondage of exteriority. Description is banished that beautiful things may be evoked, magically; the regular beat of verse is broken in order that words might fly, upon subtler wings. Mystery is no longer to be feared ... We are coming closer to nature, as we seem to shrink from it with something of horror, disdaining to catalogue the trees of the forest. And as we brush aside the accidents of daily life ... we come closer to humanity.[27]

For Symons, the revolution effected by the Symbolists is, therefore, partly a formal one, breaking with traditional form and rhythmic regularity in poetry in order to release and to present 'beautiful things' more powerfully.

Symons's general principles, therefore, look forward to the dictates of the movement which Ezra Pound, H. D., and the English poet and novelist Richard Aldington created in the early summer of 1912, Imagism, as a means of focusing and promoting the shared aspects of their work. (Imagism was originally 'Imagisme' in Pound's use of the word, signalling the French origins of the ideas, but also lending a fake sophistication to the movement.) Pound later retrospectively offered three characteristics of Imagist poetry: 'Direct treatment of the "thing" whether subjective or objective'; 'To use absolutely no word which does not contribute to the presentation'; 'As regarding rhythm: to compose in the sequence of the musical phrase, not in sequence of the metronome'.[28] True, Pound's other definition of the Image, as an 'intellectual and emotional complex in an instant of time', is wary, in its psychological suggestiveness, of that 'spiritual' and 'magical' aspect of poetry which Symons discovered for English poetry in the French Symbolists. Yet, at the same time, the shared qualities between the Image and the Symbol of the Symbolists are direct, and carry implications for the relation of the poet to their work. Moreover, the relation which poetic work in the Imagist mode makes with its readers became characteristic of the modernist enterprise more broadly.

Symons seems to find the most intense rendition of the Symbolist ambition in the work of Mallarmé, in whose work he finds that

> The word, treated indeed with a kind of 'adoration', as [Mallarmé] says, is so regarded in a magnificent sense, in which it is apprehended as a living thing, itself the vision rather than the reality . . . The word . . . is for him a liberating principle, by which the spirit is extracted from matter.[29]

In Mallarmé's poetry, in other words, language itself becomes a spiritual quantity with a live force and freshness, as though it had never been used before. The reader is taken away from the realm of the everyday into a state of visionary intensity. In this process, language is seen as engulfing the poet himself. The traditional version of the poetic lyric, in which the personal voice of the poet is to be heard through the poem, is overturned. In Mallarmé's poetry what we hear instead is, for Symons, the spiritual, immortal quality of language itself. The poet is a mediator of these magical qualities, not an author or establisher of meaning in the world of the text as hitherto. Symons's ideas here look forward again to some characteristics of Imagist verse, and also to the notions of the necessary 'impersonality' of the artist developed in the late 1910s and early 1920s by T. S. Eliot. This he formulated most famously in 'Tradition and the Individual Talent': 'Poetry is not the turning loose of emotion, but an escape from emotion; it is not the expression of personality, but an escape from personality.'[30] Through poetry, in other words, the personal feelings and the everyday social character of the poet are left behind. Eliot's 'escape' here reads like a later version of Symons's notion of words in poetry taking flight.

As suggested above, the contemporary poetic exemplar of Symons's Symbolist aesthetic writing in English was the Anglo-Irishman, W. B. Yeats. Yeats's poetry of the 1890s had, indeed, been developing a notion of the symbolic power of poetry similar to that given classic formulation in Symons's 1899 book. Indeed, there is a sense in which Symons and Yeats were developing, by the late 1890s, their ideas about poetry through conversation and mutual influence. Yeats, for instance, claimed that Symons's 1898 translations of some poems by Mallarmé inspired some of the 'latter poems' of his own 1899 collection *The Wind Among the Reeds*.[31] It is true that there are Symbolist features in parts of the sequence meditating upon love and its loss towards the end of Yeats's book, as for example in 'He wishes for the Cloths of Heaven': 'Had I the heavens' embroidered cloths . . . I would spread the cloths beneath your feet: / But I, being poor, have only my dreams'.[32] The natural aspects of the sky are powerfully displaced here by the symbolic 'cloths', and by the imaginative act of placing them for the lover to 'tread' upon. The poem ironically and self-consciously pitches the poetic imagination ('dreams') on a par with a godly possession over the changing world, and, in the act of symbolizing that world, manifests similar power and possession.

Some years earlier in this decade Yeats's work had already consistently established a similar pitch. In 'To the Rose upon the Rood of Time' of about 1892, for example, he interweaves elements of Irish mythology with a personal mythology of a worldly eternal beauty (p. 31):

> Red rose, proud Rose, sad Rose of all my days!
> Come near me, while I sing the ancient ways:
> Cuchulain battling with the bitter tide;
> The Druid, grey, wood-nurtured, quiet-eyed,
> Who cast round Fergus dreams, and ruin untold;
> And thine own sadness.

Yeats's invoked symbolic Rose becomes a muse and a yearned-for perfection, a freshness and originality which has outlived even the stars. Yeats's project, in these 1890s collections of poetry, is one that seeks to establish his native literary and mythological Irish tradition as fit subject – one marking its distinction from the subjects of English work. The unexplained occurrence of Cuchulain, 'the Druid', and Fergus, all figures from Irish mythology, is part of this. It is a project caught up with Yeats's interest in mysticism and esoteric knowledge, as well as with displaced reference to his personal life. The rose also symbolizes his ideal love, Maud Gonne, as a kind of incarnation of Ireland itself. In the latter part of 'To the Rose upon the Rood of Time', Yeats momentarily recognizes the danger of acceding too fully to the poetic, visionary, and symbolic world which he has established for himself, suggesting that it threatens to overwhelm the everyday and natural worlds. He returns, however, by the end of the poem, to his invocation of the Rose, and to his set purpose in seeking through its inspiration to recover the ancient stories of his country: 'I would, before my time to go, / Sing of old Eire and the ancient ways'.

That sense of modern poetic returning through symbol and story to the ancient past is key, also, to the later Imagist project. When the ambitious young American poet Ezra Pound arrived in London in 1908, Yeats was the poet he most wanted to meet, and the two poets remained interlocutors for many years about the nature of modern poetry.[33] Pound's 'The Return', a poem first published in that same early summer of 1912 in which he was discussing Imagism with H. D. and Aldington, manifests that recovery of mythological possibility in a classical context which Yeats had achieved in the local setting for his poems of the 1890s:

> See, they return; ah, see the tentative
> Movements, and the slow feet,
> The trouble in the pace and the uncertain
> Wavering![34]

Pound's poem envisions the hesitant re-emergence of some fictional (but presumably modelled on Greek) gods into the world. As with Yeats's 'The Rose . . .', the subject of the poem is deeply ambiguous and recondite – 'they' are compared by Pound both to snow and to 'souls of blood' which harry and raven on humanity. The Image realized through the poetry is immediate but at the same time remote – remote both from the intimate concerns of the poet and from those of the reader, manifesting rather a version of that terrible but eternal beauty which is the subject of Yeats's symbolism.

Pound was later to distance Imagism from Symbolism, claiming that a 'symbolist's *symbols* have a fixed value' whereby the moon, for instance, carries a set of absolute metonymic referents – coldness, variability, etc. For Pound, Imagism is more suggestive, opening a multitude of possible interpretations for its reader. The effectiveness of this distinction is debatable, however, given, as I have been arguing, the range of new possibilities Yeats finds in the traditional symbol of the rose, and the obvious reference of Pound's images in 'The Return'. But Pound's own distinction needs respect.[35] Moreover, he was perhaps aware of this problem of divergent readings and he sought to resolve it in his ready embrace of a new version of modern art in the days before the outbreak of World War One. This was an art embodied in the 'Vorticism' associated with Wyndham Lewis's magazine *Blast* (discussed in Chapter 3).

Lawrence Rainey has argued that Pound was anxious to invent a 'movement' which he called Imagism because he had become perturbed that hugely popular theatrical events being staged at the time in London by the poet, performer, and propagandist of an Italian movement called Futurism, Filippo Marinetti, threatened to take attention away from the aesthetic values to which Pound himself held.[36] Futurism, as Marinetti saw it, celebrated the immediate and contemporary through its appropriation of the dynamics and speed of modern technology and communications – cars, aeroplanes, telephones. The traditional distinctions between works of art and those facets of life which seemed to compromise aesthetic values were here swept away. Pound, in reaction with Imagist works like 'The Return', now promulgated instead a belated version of poetic symbolism in which poetry, reluctantly and uncertainly but magisterially, comes back into contact with its ancient origins and (metrically as well as ideologically) rediscovers its connections with a numinous and spiritual possibility.

Rainey emphasizes the fact that Pound's resistance is partly founded upon his belief in the nobility and exclusivity of the best art. His engagement is with a small elite audience, which is particularly attuned with his aesthetic ambition rather than with the popular audience drawn to Marinetti. That resistance is particularly present in the ambition developed by Pound and Yeats, partly in collaboration during the years of the First World War, to resurrect an ancient form of drama from Japan, the Noh theatre. In its recourse to ancient myths and stories, Pound's and Yeats's interest in this theatre is continuous with some of the ambitions they shared through their personal versions of Symbolism and Imagism. Drama is the literary form which showed the most resilience to the kinds of formal experiment which elsewhere characterized modernist novels and poems.[37] In the theatre works by these two poets performed in the drawing-rooms of the rich, however, the ideas behind the dramatic encounters between present and past in the poetry were brought startlingly to life.

For Pound, in his introduction to his translation of some of the Noh plays, the 'game' was not merely for the audience (both ancient and contemporary) to know which of the plays was which,

> but to give each one of them a beautiful and allusive name, to recall by the title some strange event of history or some passage of romance or

legend. It was a refinement in barbarous times . . . The art of allusion, or this love of allusion in art, is at the root of the Noh.[38]

Pound's emphasis upon the glories of allusiveness in this theatre looks forward to his compatriot T. S. Eliot's thinking on the nature of modern art in his essays of the early 1920s and his practice in his modernist 'epic' *The Waste Land* (1922). But the praise of that 'refinement in barbarous times' which the theatre instils in its exclusive and knowledgeable audience of course carried resonance in Pound's own times, where the barbarities of the Western Front in the First World War were being daily reported in the newspapers. Yeats's 1916 essay on 'Certain Noble Plays of Japan' shows the degree of collaboration between the two poets in presenting this oblique aesthetic possibility as a form of resistance to the contemporary catastrophe. Yeats emphasizes the artificiality of the Noh theatre and its difference from the realism which predominates in the 'popular arts':

> No 'naturalistic' effect is sought. The players wear masks and found their movements upon those of puppets . . . A swift or a slow movement and a long or short stillness, and then another movement. They sing as much as they speak . . . At the climax, instead of the disordered passion of nature, there is a dance, a series of positions and movements which may represent a battle, or a marriage . . . The interest is not in the human form but in the rhythm to which it moves, and the triumph of their art is to express the rhythm in its intensity.[39]

Yeats makes the context of his essay more explicit than Pound ('The Print Room of the British Museum is now closed as a war-economy, so I can only write from memory'). But, like Pound, he sees the artificiality of the Noh drama as offering some redemptive possibility at this historical moment. As so many 'human forms' are being arbitrarily destroyed on the battlefield, he envisages a world in which the musical rhythm of dance and singing overcomes individual physicality. Instead of a realistic representation of battle, he advocates a representation of it in dance. Starting with *At the Hawk's Well* in 1917, Yeats's work on the Noh can be seen to have had a controlling impact upon his own play-writing. The play centres upon the figures of an old and a young man as they seek the waters of the well, waters that are said to bestow immortality on anyone who drinks of them. It shows Yeats dramatizing the tensions within his view of the potency of myth and legend, as exemplified in both his Symbolist poetry and his interest in the Japanese plays, during this time of war. The Old Man has spent his whole life waiting for the waters along with 'a solitary girl among the rocks'. But the avenging spirit of the hawk, into which the girl is transformed at the end, guards the well. Both old and young man miss the flowing of the waters, and the play ends with an irruption of violence: 'What are those cries? / . . . Who are they that beat a sword upon a shield? / . . . The clash of arms again!'[40]

At the Hawk's Well offers, in other words, an equal and opposing resolution to that envisaged by Yeats and Pound in their promotion of the Noh drama. Instead of being fruitful, the legend of the well proves to be a delusion for those humans who are unable to benefit from its potential. War and avenging violence lurk in the background, waiting to destroy the illusion. Pound and Yeats's venture into drama at this time, therefore, dramatizes the self-conscious frailties of that aestheticism which had underwritten their earlier explorations of the relation between modernity and tradition, the contemporary and the ancient past. The tensions between the aesthetic and history at the time of World War One will form the subject of Chapter 3. But we can see here that a principal strategy for modernist writing was to seek to translate contemporary barbarous violence into symbolic and oblique narratives, which both resist and comment upon the 'disordered passion' of the historical context.

Imperial encounters and modernism

Pound and Yeats's interest in the formal and narrative possibilities of the Noh theatre exemplifies modernism's interest not only in other historical moments which might act as parallels to the contemporary, but also the frequent recourse to other cultures which might provide analogies or resistance. Such possibilities of new imaginative and (sometimes) spiritual possibility had already been explored across the 1890s in other modes beyond the Symbolist one, modes that similarly continued to have an impact on modernist literature. It is striking that a number of key modernist texts are, for instance, haunted by colonial experience, and by the possibilities of encounter with cultures and religions beyond established cultural reference points in Western Europe. As the historian Eric Hobsbawm has maintained, 1875–1914 formed 'the age of empire'. It was a time in which 'it became clear that the society and civilization created by and for the Western liberal bourgeoisie represented not the permanent form of the modern industrial world, but only one phase of its early development'.[41]

The social stability which had marked the nineteenth century was giving way not just to the disturbing questioning offered by socialism and the movement for women's rights, but also by the paradoxical colonial experience itself. As Chapter 4 will argue, writing by, amongst others, Eliot, Pound, E. M. Forster, Woolf, and Lawrence establishes knowledge and

experience from outside Europe as part of the nexus of new and often disturbing possibilities which they wish to explore.[42] This is true of Woolf's
The Years, as has been shown above, but it is also true of other texts which
have come to be read against the backdrop of radical possibilities of the
modernist moment. These possibilities go far in establishing the disturbing
potentiality of the imperial encounter in even traditionally recognizable
literary contexts. The previous section of this chapter has concentrated on
the questioning of individuality across this period. What we find in
modernist works that include some sense of engagement with imperial
history and government is a similar sense that selfhood and character are
unsettled by it. Characters with experience of empire, in their turn, unsettle
the social conventions of England when they return home. This has an
impact upon the formal aspects of modernist work. As readers, we are
unable to define and contain our sense of these characters' nature.

D. H. Lawrence's late novel *Lady Chatterley's Lover*, for instance, is
often perceived as having notoriously challenged the English class system
through its suggestion that desire recognizes no social boundaries. Connie
Chatterley's affair with the gamekeeper Oliver Mellors allows Lawrence to
stage a new rhetorical explicitness about sex which breaks through the
established conventions of the marriage-novel as it had been explored in the
late nineteenth century and into the twentieth. What has perhaps been less
remarked upon is the social mobility of Mellors himself – the fact that he
(like other figures we have already discussed) presents a variety of selves to
the world, depending on the society in which he appears. The famous thick
dialect words in which he utters his rawest celebration of sex is an assumed
voice, and his switch back and forth between received pronunciation and
dialect is part of the unnerving potentiality within English society which
Lawrence perceives to have resulted from the First World War.[43]

Yet the novel also reminds us that Mellors's ability to act the part, to play
on vocal and social possibility, despite his seeming provincialism, depends
largely upon his having seen army service on the north-west frontier in
India, where, as Clifford patronizingly conceded, 'he may have picked up
certain tricks' (p. 68). At other points we are told that Mellors is 'very well
informed' about India, and we see him reading a book about it; Clifford also
concedes that after such an experience (Mellors became ill there), he must
have found it difficult to return to England and readapt to its society (pp.
282, 120, 92). Mellors's refusal to acknowledge the 'normal' boundaries
long established within English class-bound society, in other words, and his
consequent spontaneity, are implicitly associated with his recent experience
of the colonial space – one which renders him an outsider upon his return.
Like Woolf in *The Years*, Lawrence in this post-war state-of-England novel

sees the shifting, if not unstable, nature and consciousness of the nation itself as relating to its colonial history. The radical disturbance caused in particular local and social contexts is seen as here being brought about by that regular experience of ruling the empire. And this has immediate formal consequences for the novel itself, in the shifting, ambiguous perspectives and modes of voice in the book.

Such formal disturbances had often surfaced in fiction from the Victorian period relating to empire (think of Wilkie Collins's *The Moonstone* or Charles Dickens's *The Mystery of Edwin Drood*, for example). But they had perhaps intensified in the 1880s and 1890s with the popularity of H. Rider Haggard, Robert Louis Stevenson, Rudyard Kipling, and the more technical (and much less commercially successful) literary developments in narrative form effected by Joseph Conrad. Conrad's significance has already been suggested by my discussion of Woolf above; but he was an immensely significant figure in the period, as witnessed by, for instance, the epigraph to Eliot's *The Hollow Men*. The British imperialist Kipling seems a less immediately crucial precursor for modernism, yet, for example, Eliot relished Kipling's writing from his childhood reading in Boston, and went on to edit, in 1941, *A Choice of Kipling's Verse*. Eliot's compatriot Pound went so far as to claim that Kipling's 'sheer force of content, of tale to tell' meant he was more likely to endure as a writer than the literary master, Henry James.[44]

Some of the mixture of styles I will describe in Pound and Eliot's work later in this book, a mixing of 'high' and 'low' idioms, is predicted in the proto-modernist style and formal incompleteness of Kipling. Kipling frequently and ironically stages the colonial encounter as a clash between colonial and professional hierarchies and the realities of life in India in ways that will become familiar across the modernist period. His confident writing hovers in an uncertain zone between journalism and literature, fact and fiction, in ways that illustrate the unsettling of definitions and boundaries which the stories themselves often describe at the level of content. As the narrator of 'The Madness of Private Ortheris' from *Plain Tales from the Hills* (first English edition, 1890) comically concludes, 'I could not come to any conclusion of any kind whatever.'[45]

The narrative voice in these stories is often difficult to locate, unidentifiable, and in no superior position of knowledge to that of the protagonist's. That problem over narrative completion, voice, and distance arising from the colonial encounter the stories manifest, marks the originality of Kipling's writing. One of the oddest of the stories, 'The Strange Ride of Morrowbie Jukes', for example, starts off by undermining the exact veracity of its own narrative. The story tells of a journey into the Indian desert by the British civil engineer Jukes, a journey which ends mysteriously as he becomes incarcerated in a pit at what seems to be a kind of Hindu punishment camp. The 'reality' of this incident is itself questionable, as the first-person narrative in which Jukes tells of it admits that he was suffering from an attack of fever at the time. Is the story, then, an hallucination? Matters are rendered even more ambiguous in the version collected in the 1888 volume by Kipling, *The Phantom Rickshaw*. There, an anonymous introducer of Jukes's 'tale' opens by dubiously over-asserting that 'There is no invention about this tale' – Kipling's joke on his audience. The veracity of the tale is asserted by this anonymous speaker because Jukes 'never varies the tale in the telling'. But he immediately contradicts this: 'He wrote this quite straightforwardly at first, but he has touched it up in places and introduced Moral Reflections.'[46]

No less than in 'high' modernist texts like Eliot's own *The Waste Land*, texts similarly interrupted by voices of uncertain provenance, then, we find in Kipling's tales of imperial administration a distinctive unsettling of literary characterization and formal convention. Related issues around literary form, and its relation to uncertain knowledge in the colonial encounter, recur in the 1890s' writing of Joseph Conrad. Conrad's 'Author's Note' to his first novel, *Almayer's Folly* (1895) asserts the common humanity of all the peoples of the earth: 'common mortals, no matter where they live; in houses or in huts, in the streets under a fog, or in the forests behind the dark line of dismal mangroves that fringe the vast solitude of the sea.'[47] Yet the progress of the narrative plots the Dutch trader Almayer's degeneration as he seeks to establish himself between competing inter-racial feuds, in his own cross-racial marriage, and in the pressures of the international market. Conrad suggests again the failure of the imperial enterprise and of global capitalism which underlies it.[48] Almayer's 'folly', the house he seeks to build on the banks of an equatorial river, remains incomplete and uninhabited by the end of the book, a symbol of the ultimate powerlessness of the colonizers in the alien habitat. Like Jukes, then, Almayer loses his sense of himself in a different, but related, colonial circumstance.

Heart of Darkness, the novella serialized between 1898 and 1899, proved the culmination of this early range of Conrad's imperial preoccupations. Its narrative of quest, in which the narrator Marlow recounts his voyage up the Congo River in search of the missing colonial officer Kurtz, is framed by descriptions in which the 'darkness' revealed in that journey is remapped back onto the twin imperial centres, London and Brussels. Marlow relates what a further narrator of the tale calls 'one of his inconclusive experiences' whilst on a boat afloat in the river Thames. Gesturing at the city of London around, Marlow asserts famously that 'this also ... has been one of the dark places of the earth'.[49] The decadence and horror which is revealed by the encounter with Kurtz, who has invented his own hideously parodic version of civilization and Christian religion in the jungle, also lies somewhere under the pavements of the city, and in the psyches of its inhabitants. Kurtz's own 'degradation' of the imperial idea leads him to a shadowed, haunted use of language, 'the terrific suggestiveness of words heard in dreams' (p. 107), which is also a 'withering of one's belief in mankind', a failure of all attempts to narrate its history. Marlow, as the teller of Kurtz's tale to the 'civilized' world, cannot himself convey the reality he has seen into on his quest (p. 50):

> it is impossible to convey the life-sensation of any given epoch of one's existence, – that which makes its truth, its meaning – its subtle and penetrating essence. It is impossible. We live, as we dream – alone.

As his story progresses, therefore, Marlow speaking in the darkness of the night on the river becomes little more than a voice out of a void. His is a disembodied 'narrative that seemed to shape itself without human lips', and in many ways he is simply a more 'civilized' version of Kurtz, who becomes an alter ego (p. 80):

> He was very little more than a voice. And I heard – him – it – this voice – other voices – all of them were so little more than voices – and the memory of that time itself lingers around me, impalpable, like a dying vibration of one immense jabber.

Conrad's conclusion from his various renditions of imperial adventure and cross-racial relationship by the end of the 1890s would seem to be, therefore, that fictional narrative required new modes of expression in order to render fully the various dislocations that colonial adventure entailed. Rod Edmond has argued that the progression of Conrad's writing from the 1890s into his later work is one in which degeneration threatens not just the metropolitan/imperial but also the colonized spaces, and that in the process the hierarchies between cultural centre and 'savage' margin are threatened. This is then the key lesson Conrad relays to later writers such as T. S. Eliot.[50] Yet also under threat in these tales is the very possibility of coherent expression, of textual completion, in rendering that colonial encounter, as the conventional centres of kernels of meaning-construction deteriorate before the content of the narrative. Conrad's famous boxes-within-boxes narratives simply enclose the incoherent 'heart' of modern, late imperial consciousness, a 'history' of civilization which is in fact a recurrent degradation and despair.

Notes

1 *The Years*, edited by Jeri Johnson (Harmondsworth, 1998), pp. 78–9.
2 W. E. B. Dubois, 'The Negro Mind Reaches Out', in *The New Negro*, edited by Alain Locke (New York, 1925; 1992 edition), p. 386.
3 Whilst this study will continually draw upon correlative European movements and ideas in literature and the arts to those detailed, my emphasis in a book of this size will inevitably be upon the contexts of works in English.
4 John Stevenson, *British Society 1914–45* (London, 1984), p. 23.
5 *London 1900: The Imperial Metropolis* (New Haven, 1999), pp. 93ff.
6 Jose Harris, *Private Lives, Public Spirit: Britain 1870–1914* (Harmondsworth, 1993), p. 21–2.
7 Shari Benstock, *Women of the Left Bank, Paris 1900–1940* (London, 1987).
8 *Introduction to American Studies*, edited by Malcolm Bradbury and Howard Temperley, third edition (London, 1998), pp. 178–9.
9 Carola M. Kaplan and Anne B. Simpson, *Seeing Double: Revisioning Edwardian and Modernist Literature* (Basingstoke, 1996), p. xvi.
10 *Outside Modernism: In Pursuit of the English Novel, 1900–30*, edited by Lynne Hapgood and Nancy L. Paxton (Basingstoke, 2000), p. vii.
11 Thomas Hardy, *Tess of the D'Urbervilles* (Harmondsworth, 1998), p. 124.
12 See also Smith's *The Origins of Modernism: Eliot, Pound, Yeats and the Rhetorics of Renewal* (Hemel Hempstead, 1994), pp. 1–21.
13 See, for example, Tim Redman, *Ezra Pound and Italian Fascism* (Cambridge, 1991); Paul Morrison, *The Poetics of Fascism: Ezra Pound, T. S. Eliot, Paul de Man* (New York, 1996).
14 See, for instance, Nathalie Blondel's *Mary Butts: Scenes from the Life* (New York, 1998), and Suzanne Raitt's *May Sinclair: A Modern Victorian* (Oxford, 2000).
15 See Eric Hobsbawm, *The Age of Empire 1875–1914* (London, 1987), pp. 262–75, and Jose Harris's Chapter 8, 'Society and Social Theory', in *Private Lives*.
16 Many critics, including Michael Levinson in *A Genealogy of Modernism: A Study of English Literary Doctrine 1908–1922* (Cambridge, 1984), James Longenbach in *Modernist Poetics of History: Pound, Eliot and the Sense of the Past* (Princeton, 1987), and Sanford Schwartz in *The Matrix of Modernism: Pound, Eliot and Early Twentieth-Century Thought* (Princeton, 1985), have pointed to the continuities between some aspects of late nineteenth-century thought and that of early modernists.
17 Walter Pater, *The Renaissance: Studies in Art and Poetry*, edited by Adam Phillips (Oxford, 1986), pp. 151–2.
18 Harris, *Private Lives*, p. 13.
19 Oscar Wilde, *The Portrait of Dorian Gray*, edited by Robert Mighall (Harmondsworth, 2000), pp. 9–10.
20 Declan Kiberd, *Inventing Ireland* (London, 1995), pp. 33–51.
21 A similar conclusion about the unresolved relation of art and the personality of the artist to life had been drawn in a novel by the Anglophile American Henry James in the year before *The Portrait of Dorian Gray*. James's *The Tragic Muse* (1890) contains much of the paraphernalia of Wilde's novel – the world of the stage and an actress, an artist, a decadent critic, even a Gray-like portrait which 'the hand of time was rubbing ... away little by little' (edited by Philip Horne (Harmondsworth, 1995), p. 476).
22 Sally Ledger, 'The New Woman and the Crisis of Victorianism', in *Cultural Politics at the Fin de Siècle*, edited by Sally Ledger and Scott McCracken (Cambridge, 1995), p. 24.

23 Quoted in the introduction to George Egerton, *Keynotes and Discords* (1893–4) (London, 1983), p. xv.

24 Karl Beckson, *Arthur Symons: A Life* (Oxford, 1987), p. 35.

25 *Selected Prose of T. S. Eliot*, edited by Frank Kermode (London, 1975), p. 52.

26 *Selected Letters of Ezra Pound 1907–1941*, edited by D. D. Paige (London, 1950), p. 218. The influence of Hulme, whom Pound met at the Poet's Club in 1909, was crucial to his own ideas on Imagism and his later interest in the visual arts just before the First World War. In essays like 'Romanticism and Classicism' of 1911 or 1912, Hulme drew a key philosophical distinction between the romantic's belief that 'man, the individual, is an infinite reservoir of possibilities' and the contradictory classical belief that 'Man is an extraordinarily fixed and limited animal . . . It is only by tradition and organization that anything decent can be got out of him . . . The classical poet never forgets this finiteness, this limit of man.' The classical belief in man's limitation through 'original sin' also influenced the religious writing of T. S. Eliot. See *T. E. Hulme: Selected Writings*, edited by Patrick McGuinness (Manchester, 1998), pp. 70–1.

27 Arthur Symons, *The Symbolist Movement in Literature*, second revised edition (London, 1908), p. 8. Compare, for example, Pound's disdainful dismissal of Tennyson as the typical English poet writing 'pretty embroideries' in 'The Rev. G. Crabbe, LL.B', *Literary Essays of Ezra Pound*, edited by T. S. Eliot (London, 1954), p. 277.

28 Pound, 'A Retrospect', in *Literary Essays*, p. 3.

29 Symons, *The Symbolist Movement in Literature*, p. 126.

30 *Selected Prose of T. S. Eliot*, p. 43. In *The Symbolist Movement in Literature*, it is Jules Laforgue who exemplifies most tellingly the adaptability of this aesthetic to modern life – its contemporaneity. Symons sees there 'the haste to escape from whatever weighs too heavily on the liberty of the moment' (p. 108), and Laforgue's mixture of an ironical detachment from the details of everyday with pity is echoed in some of Eliot's early *personae*, most famously J. Alfred Prufrock.

31 Yeats, *Autobiographies* (London, 1955), p. 320. See also Stéphane Mallarmé, *Poésies*, translated by Arthur Symons, selected and edited by Bruce Morris (Edinburgh, 1986), p. 19.

32 *The Collected Poems of W. B. Yeats: A New Edition*, edited by Richard Finneran (Basingstoke, 1983), p. 73.

33 Noel Stock, *The Life of Ezra Pound* (Harmondsworth, 1985), p. 84. Helen Carr has noted that not only Yeats but other Irish nationalist poets were important to Pound as he was beginning to formulate the ideas leading to Imagism. Joseph Campbell and Desmond Fitzgerald were part of the small group of poets who met at the Tour Eiffel in London's Soho in 1909–10. As a result of all of these influences, Pound's voice when reading his own poetry sounded with an Irish accent across his life. See Helen Carr, 'Imagism and Empire', in *Modernism and Empire*, edited by Howard J. Booth and Nigel Rigby (Manchester, 2000), pp. 75ff.

34 *Collected Early Poems of Ezra Pound*, edited by Michael John King (New York, 1976), p. 198. Yeats's admiration for 'The Return' is exhibited in his inclusion of it in his 1936 anthology, *The Oxford Book of Modern Verse 1892–1935*, and his singling out of the work for discussion in its introduction.

35 Ezra Pound, *Gaudier-Brzeska* (New York, 1970), p. 84.

36 Lawrence Rainey, *Institutions of Modernism: Literary Elites and Popular Culture* (New Haven, 1998), p. 12.

37 As Steven Watson has maintained, the only other claimant to having invented a modernist theatre beyond Pound and Yeats would be the coterie centred upon

the Provincetown Players in the same war years, a coterie from which emerged the work of Eugene O'Neill. See *Strange Bedfellows: The First American Avant-Garde* (New York, 1991), pp. 212–24.

38 *The Translations of Ezra Pound*, with an introduction by Hugh Kenner (London, 1953), p. 214.

39 W. B. Yeats, *Essays and Introductions* (London, 1961), pp. 230–1. James Longenbach, in *Stone Cottage* (Oxford, 1988), has written an excellent account of the collaboration between the two poets on the Noh across the war years.

40 *The Collected Plays of W. B. Yeats* (London, 1982), p. 218.

41 Hobsbawm, *The Age of Empire*, pp. 9–11.

42 Elleke Boehmer, in *Empire, the National and the Postcolonial 1890–1920* (Oxford, 2002), engages with this nexus more fully.

43 See D. H. Lawrence, *Lady Chatterley's Lover*, edited by Michael Squires (Harmondsworth, 2000), pp. 46–7.

44 Pound, *Literary Essays*, p. 323.

45 Rudyard Kipling, *Plain Tales from the Hills* (London, 1994), p. 296.

46 Rudyard Kipling, *Wee Willie Winkie*, edited by Hugh Haughton (Harmondsworth, 1988), p. 186.

47 Joseph Conrad, *Almayer's Folly*, edited by Jacques Berthoud (Oxford, 1992), p. lxii.

48 In its sense of the progressive corruption of the white imperialists before the straitened realities of colonial existence, Conrad's early fiction echoes the South Sea tales of Robert Louis Stevenson, particularly perhaps 'The Beach at Falesá', published originally in 1892.

49 Joseph Conrad, *Heart of Darkness*, edited by Robert Hampson (Harmondsworth, 1995), p. 18.

50 Rod Edmond, 'Degeneration in Imperialist and Modernist Discourse', in *Modernism and Empire*, pp. 45, 54, 59.

|2|

Modernism, cities, and societies

The late nineteenth and early twentieth centuries saw the consequences of a radical shift in population, and consequently in political focus, society, and culture, in both Europe and America. In 1800, only seventeen European cities contained over 100,000 people; by 1890, 103 did. London in the early nineteenth century was the largest city in Europe; by the end, Paris, Vienna, and Berlin had joined it in having over a million inhabitants. Both Europe and America were rapidly becoming less dependent on rural economies. As a consequence, all of the major industrial nations were experiencing a new phenomenon. An apparently rootless urban labouring class was becoming the majority population.[1] In the large cities, a sharp delineation existed between those areas which housed manual workers in poor conditions, and the more affluent middle and lower-middle classes in the suburbs. Such inequalities fuelled the rise of socialist movements in the latter years of the nineteenth century, movements often driven by ideas from those who were themselves provided for by independent means, as in the Fabian partnership of Sidney and Beatrice Webb in London.

The rise of middle-class affluence bought with it a new audience for the arts. On the other hand, the new social mix in the cities allowed for a greater blend of cultural possibility. The new 'popular' arts, such as cinema and jazz, had an immediate impact upon the former 'high' arts of literature and classical music. The European capital cities of London and Paris provided a cultural lure (and a potential space of personal and sexual freedom) for Americans seeking to escape the comparative provincialism of their own country at the time. For a variety of cultural and political reasons, individuals from within Britain and Ireland were drawn to London. There arose across these years, therefore, an increasing number of literary and artistic coteries in the cities which reflected a broader national mix than hitherto. For instance, the dinners held to encourage discussion between poets at the

Tour Eiffel restaurant in Soho, London, in 1909 were attended by the American Ezra Pound. The debates there had a clear impact upon his development of the ideas behind Imagism, discussed in the previous chapter. Yet those events were attended also by the Irish nationalist poets Joseph Campbell and Desmond Fitzgerald, and hosted by the English, Cambridge-educated T. E. Hulme and the working-class autodidact F. S. Flint. This chapter will discuss the impact of new metropolitan life, and of cosmopolitanism, upon modernist culture and literature, whilst doing so in the light of the debates about individuality and aesthetics raised in Chapter 1. T. S. Eliot names Vienna and London in *The Waste Land* as 'unreal' cities. Where does that sense of unreality arise from?

London

In Robert Louis Stevenson's *The Strange Case of Dr Jekyll and Mr Hyde* (1886), Mr Hyde, the alter ego of the experimental scientist Dr Jekyll, commits the brutal murder of Sir Danvers Carew in a London street, 'a crime of singular ferocity'. Mr Utterson, a lawyer friend of Jekyll, sets out in pursuit of the murderer, having recognized that the murder weapon is a stick that he had given to the doctor:

> Mr Utterson beheld a marvellous number of degrees and hues of twilight; for here it would be dark like the back-end of evening; and there would be a glow of a rich, lurid brown, like the light of some strange conflagration . . . The dismal quarter of Soho seen under these changing glimpses, with its muddy ways, and slatternly passengers, and its lamps, which had never been extinguished or had been kindled afresh to combat this mournful reinvasion of darkness, seemed, in the lawyer's eyes, like a district of some city in a nightmare. The thoughts of his mind, besides, were of the gloomiest dye.[2]

Stevenson's character experiences the city during his pursuit of Hyde as a bleak, foggy place, reminiscent of the opening of Dickens's *Bleak House*. For Dickens, though, the murkiness of the city streets reflects symbolically the elusive and self-servingly obscure legal world which holds the fate of the novel's characters in its grip through the seemingly interminable case of *Jarndyce* v. *Jarndyce*. With Stevenson's description of Soho after the murder, however, the vision of the city streets is no longer harnessed as a vehicle with which to criticize one of the institutions of state. The 'changing glimpses' of the city's fabric through the fog, the alternating darkness and light of a 'strange conflagration' ('strange' in direct echo of the novel's title), are rather here directly linked to the 'nightmare' entailed by the schizophrenic personality shifts of the novel's central persona.

The 'gloomiest dye' of Utterson's thoughts seems to reflect his perceptions of the city on his journey through it. But it also serves to *create* those perceptions, through his dawning intimation of some link between his friend Jekyll and his demonic counterpart, Hyde. The city takes on aspects of the polymorphous identity of the protagonist, who, as Hyde, leaves his lair through a 'blistered and disdained' door in 'a sinister block of building' in a small street (p. 30). The city, in other words, provides perfect cover for such threatening forces. Here, as in other late Victorian Gothic renditions of the city such as those in Sir Arthur Conan Doyle's Sherlock Holmes story *The Sign of Four* (1890) or Bram Stoker's 1897 pot-boiler, *Dracula*, the fabric of the city provides the outward expression of the psychology of the protagonists. The novel uses description of the city primarily as a means to *psychologize*. Such popular fictional renditions in their turn look forward to the high literary experiments of modernist writers such as Eliot and Woolf, as this chapter will show.

The fictional representation of London in 'high' literature towards the turn of the century was one in which the predominant social mobility leaves the central characters in difficult or tragic circumstances. In *What Maisie Knew* (1897), the American novelist Henry James examines the precarious situation of a child shuttled between divorced parents; in his *The Awkward Age* (1899), he follows the fraught emergence of a modern young woman into a London social scene dominated by literary salons. The Englishman George Gissing, in *New Grub Street* (1891), had directly addressed the difficult situation of the modern writer in these perplexing modern circumstances. Gissing charts the vicissitudes of a group of people seeking to survive through their labours in the literary world, and principally the contrast in destiny between Jasper Milvain, the timeserver who is able to produce literary articles for magazines on the latest topics of the day, and Reardon, his friend. Reardon aspires to be a recognized literary novelist, yet is unable to equate his ambition with the need to provide for his wife and young child. Across the novel he sinks deeper and deeper into despair and poverty, finally leaves his family, and dies in abjection.

Most tellingly, Gissing maps this scene (as he does others in his other novels), and particularly the progress of Reardon's decline, exactly against actual London streets and districts. The districts in which people are situated in London provide an index to their relative social and financial situations – Marian's mother, for instance, comes from Holloway, a sure sign of her poverty and upward mobility through marriage to a house off the Camden Road.[3] Much of the novel's action, however, is situated in the relatively well-to-do streets around the British Museum, whose Library provides the hub of this literary production. This district continued to focus literary activity into the twentieth century, with movements like Imagism being 'founded' in cafés and bookshops amongst these streets, and with the eventual emergence of the Bloomsbury group of writers, based around Russell Square, in the early 1910s. Gissing's mapping of narrative onto the city streets, a mapping which presumes knowledge of the allusiveness and social and class implication involved in certain locations, looks forward to some of the key texts of modernism. Eliot's *The Waste Land*, Joyce's *Ulysses*, parts of E. M. Forster's *Howards End*, and Virginia Woolf's *Mrs Dalloway* similarly designate the city as a realistic *and* a symbolic place, and as an index of identities.

Gissing's novel is illuminating also in that it establishes literature as a modern industry in this urban space in ways that look forward to future developments. He is fascinated by the sometimes fantastical processes of literary production and commentary which sustain those, like Milvain, who are able to exploit them, but which destroy those, such as Reardon, who refuse to play by the rules. The daughter of a literary-critical family, Marian Yule, who aids her father by writing literary articles for him, at one point in the novel misreads a newspaper advertisement

> ... headed 'Literary Machine'; had it then been invented at last, some automaton to supply the place of poor creatures such as herself, to turn out books and articles? ... surely before long some Edison would make the true automaton; the problem must be comparatively such a simple one. Only to throw in a given number of old books, and have them reduced, blended, modernised into a single one for the day's consumption.[4]

Marian's eerie and troubling vision predicts not only the synthesizing nature of the modernist literary text, created from a welter of diverse materials. It also predicts that fascination with mechanism and mechanistic literary production to be found in various modernist works from Marinetti's Futurist poems to Wyndham Lewis's so-called Vorticist productions (which will be discussed in Chapter 3). At the same time, this fear at an autonomous production which disables the actual modern author looks forward to the ways in which modernist writers felt the need to seize control of the processes of dissemination with regard to their writing through the so-called 'little magazines' of their period. The key modernist 'movements', including Imagism and Vorticism in the English literary world, as well as the prominence of modernist writers amongst editors of the literary magazines of the time, furthered these attempts to wrest back the terms of debate.[5]

Across the early years of the twentieth century, the linkage between rapidly evolving London life and the identities of its commentators was ensured through a series of texts which hover, like Gissing's characters, between the worlds of literature and journalistic belles-lettres. Arthur Symons, the poet and critic whose direct knowledge of the Paris literary world in the 1890s did much to transform British, Irish, and American literary consciousness, gathered together several collections of his travel essays from journals into books, including *Cities* (1903) and *Cities and Sea Coasts* (1918). In the dedicatory preface to the former, Symons asserted that:

> I am one of those people for whom the visible world exists, very actively; and, for me, cities are like people, with souls and temperaments of their own, and it has always been one of my chief pleasures to associate with the souls and temperaments congenial to me among cities. And as love, or, it may be, hate, can alone reveal soul to soul, among human beings, so, it seems to me, the soul of the city will reveal itself only to those who love . . . For we can see or receive, in people or things, only our own part of them: the vision rising in our own eyes, the passion rising in our own hearts.[6]

Perception for Symons is largely indistinguishable from projection. This opening statement is shocking: 'I am one of those people for whom the visible world exists, very actively.' It is an anxious attempt to rebut an absolute solipsistic interiority, or a life of the mind, which subsumes all objective reality. And yet, at the same time, he realizes that the perceived life of the city is dominated by 'the passion rising in our own hearts'. Only when the map of a congenial city matches up with the uncharted territory of his own far-sighted emotion can he write about it. Interior and exterior, the external life of the city, its actual streets and buildings and, in contrast, the life of the mind which moves through the city streets, are very much in play for Symons, in fact in an irresolvable tension. It would be no good, for instance, going to Symons's book in order to find out how many people lived in the capital of England at that time. These seemingly descriptive works about European capitals by him are instead impressionistic and aesthetic accounts of the mind which reflects upon its circumstances. They do not offer the reader a set of verifiable facts.

We find a similar tension in Ford Madox Ford's *The Soul of London* (1905), the first of a trilogy of books published across three years in which Ford explores England and the English at the turn of the century. Ford shares Symons's view that the city is in itself a 'Personality' whose character he is anxious to capture in his text, as opposed to presenting a set of economic, political, and social conditions and facts. Ford is also imbued with that shared sense of the city as an interlayering of historical phases which will become key to allusive modernist texts. As he says in his introductory remarks:

> This author's endeavour should be to make the Past, the sense of all the dead Londons that have gone to the producing of this child of all the ages, like a constant ground-bass beneath the higher notes of the Present. In that way the book might, after a fashion, forecast even the Future and contain prophecies.

His text, like significant later work including *The Waste Land*, is situated self-consciously at an intermediate and transitional point between times, just as he perceives the city to be. Transition is emphasized also in Ford's 'take' upon the modern city, which he sees as 'impersonal' and an 'abstraction' whilst also being 'intimate'. Imagining the arrival of someone to dwell in the city from elsewhere in England, Ford asserts that:

> The last thing . . . he will get is any picture, any impression of London as a whole, any idea to carry about with him – of a city, in a plain, dominated by a great building . . . It is true enough to say that the dominant note of his first impression will be that of his own aloneness. It is none the less the dominant note of London.

Both long-time city dweller and new arrival, in other words, share the sense of 'London' as a place of 'innumerable trade centres, innumerable class districts', which 'becomes by its immensity a place upon which there is no beginning'. Recent technological advances, like the development of the Underground railway, had merely re-emphasized that it is impossible to perceive the city as a whole, to come to terms with the 'idea' which London is. This sense of the shared 'alone-ness' of the city's perceivers, and the inevitable partialness of their impressions of the city, then, licenses the style of Ford's book, which, like all his work, is impressionistic. Ford's sense of the infinite variety of the city occasionally draws upon sharp contrasts, such as when he weighs the likely impressions which Londoners carry with them when away from the city. Do the prismatic colours ('the green of the orange trees in tubs along the façade of the National Gallery, the vivid blue of the paper used by flower-sellers') predominate, he asks? Or is it 'the chaotic crowd . . . an apparently indissoluble muddle of gray wheel traffic', which includes the fallen, 'monstrous figure of a horse "down"' –

> And surely there is no more monstrous apparition than that of a horse down in the sticky streets with its frantic struggles, the glancing off of its hoofs, the roll of the eyes, the sudden apparition of great teeth, and then its lying still.[7]

Once again, as in late nineteenth-century texts on the city, its streets are host to impressions of a haunting grotesque ('monstrous ... apparition ... apparition') which is veiled in everyday life, but which the literary text draws our attention to ('surely there is'). There is a similar moment in the novel *The Secret Agent* (1907) by Joseph Conrad, the co-author with Ford of several books. Stevie, Conrad's child-man in the novel, is made to carry a bomb that kills him without damaging his symbolic target, the marker of the Prime Meridian, Greenwich Observatory. But Stevie is not 'mad', we are told at one point. Rather, he has 'a faithful memory of sensations'. The immediate focus of his sensitivity is the infirm horse pulling a hackney carriage: 'the ears hung at different angles, negligently; and the macabre figure of that mute dweller on the earth steamed straight up from ribs and backbone in the muggy stillness of the air'. In the bleakly cynical world of Conrad's book, though, Stevie's compassion ('"Poor! Poor!" stammered out Stevie, pushing his hands deeper into his pockets with convulsive sympathy'[8]) is further confirmation of his victimhood, and lays the path of his destruction by his cowardly and indolent brother-in-law, the secret agent himself, Mr Verloc.

Conrad's story of anarchists and revolutionaries, with its shadowy characters and indiscriminate policemen, is keyed for that vision of London which he conveyed in an Author's Note appended in 1920: 'the vision of an enormous town ... a monstrous town more populous than some continents and in its man-made might as if indifferent to heaven's frowns and smiles; a cruel devourer of the world's light' (p. 10). On a walk across London, Verloc's essential ambivalence about his situation as a revolutionary aiming to undermine the state is ironically revealed through his indolence. As he comes towards the affluent district of the city in the region of Hyde Park, Verloc concludes that 'Protection is the first necessity of opulence and luxury ... the whole social order favourable to their hygienic idleness had to be protected against the shallow enviousness of unhygienic labour' (p. 20). Part of the 'monstrousness' of Conrad's vision of the city, therefore, is the sense that there is a secret complicity between the social order and those intent upon disorder. Verloc, seemingly a respectable small shopkeeper, but actually a purveyor of pornography and agent for various anarchist and antagonistic foreign causes in the city, is in fact the man most able to move between the various sections of metropolitan society.

A similar vision of the ubiquity of the derelict and the potentially monstrous in the indifferent and anonymous city streets haunts the cityscapes in early poems by T. S. Eliot. The cat-like yellow fog and intermingled smoke that rubs along the streets of 'The Love Song of J. Alfred Prufrock' (1915) mirrors the emotional and intellectual obfuscation of the poem's central persona. A similar obscurity shrouds the city 'Under the brown fog of a winter dawn' at the end of 'The Burial of the Dead', the opening section of *The Waste Land*. This line is a translation of the medieval Italian poet Dante's vision of hell to somewhere near the contemporary London Bridge. For Eliot, as for the other authors commented on so far in this chapter, the locality in the city is both identifiable and otherwise, a multitudinous symbolic space in which the overwhelming ghostliness and unreality of modern lives are exposed. The London in *The Waste Land* is haunted by those lost on the battlefields in France during the First World War, but also by those lost in the purgatorial realm of day-to-day labour in the city, that necessity from which Verloc shrank in Conrad's novel.

Eliot's vision of the ominous cityscape is, in its turn, repeated in Virginia Woolf's *Mrs Dalloway* (1925). This is achieved not just through the repeated interjection of the phrase from Shakespeare's *Cymbeline* which Mrs Dalloway happens upon in an opened book in Hatchard's window – 'Fear no more the heat of the sun'. It is also conveyed through her sudden sense of her own bodiless unreality whilst walking along the select shopping area of Bond Street:

> She had the oddest sense of being herself invisible; unseen; unknown; there being no more marrying, no more having of children now, but only this astonishing and rather solemn progress with the rest of them.[9]

The opulent possibility of her surroundings serves further to confirm to Clarissa Dalloway that she has become detached from her essential self, and possible other and truer versions of her life. To adapt the title of Woolf's keynote essay on women, education, and writing, she has no 'room of her own', no space or place, or independent financial means, in this context where she can realize her separate individuality and potential. Like her alter ego in the book, the shell-shocked returnee from the Front, Septimus Smith, she has become detached from an earlier, pre-First World War sense of herself. That earlier self was one in which a more active life, and potential otherness of relationship – as suggested in her fascination with her friend Sally Seton – was possible. As such, the vision of London we receive through her eyes as she undertakes her shopping trip is resolutely fragmented and impressionistic:

> Bond Street fascinated her; Bond Street early in the morning in the season; its flags flying; its shops; no splash; no glitter; one roll of tweed in the shop where her father had bought his suits for fifty years; a few pearls; salmon on an iceblock.

Such prismatic impressions show, perhaps, the direct impact upon Woolf of the two Post-Impressionist exhibitions held at the Grafton Galleries, London, in 1910 and 1912.[10] These exhibitions, curated by Woolf's friend Roger Fry, introduced to the British public for the first time the works of European artists, including Paul Cézanne, Vincent van Gogh, Paul Gauguin, Henri Matisse, and Pablo Picasso. As Fry's catalogue for the second exhibition makes clear, this is an art which does not aim to 'offer a pale reflex of actual appearance, but to arouse the conviction of a new and definite reality. They do not seek to imitate form, but to create form; not to imitate life, but to find an equivalent to life.' The radical break such pictures make is from a classical tradition in which direct representation of the world is prized beyond all else. In the place of such classicism and as challenge to it, as Fry asserts, this is an 'art of associated ideas', an art which seeks to give form to the impact which the world has on its perceiver, and therefore 'its effect really depends on what we bring with us'. Such art seeks, therefore, to discover (necessarily new, since this mode of perception has not been rendered before) forms *objectively* to represent *subjective* 'reality', the flow of ideas and impressions which result from our experience of the world. Woolf's prose conjunctions in seeking to render Mrs Dalloway's impressions of the city streets, prose that pushes against the conventions of traditional active syntactical constructions, clearly shows some of these characteristics of visual art. They are central to the shift in perception, and in audience response, which her novels demand.

Whatever the familiarity of the associations conjured by the sights in the city, however, Clarissa shares in the narrative's initial shifting from one individual consciousness to another as people move through the streets. This shifting of focus coalesces around shared attempts to understand the meanings the city seems to offer to its inhabitants. This is exemplified, for instance, by the attempts to make sense, to make meaning, of the letters being spelled by the smoke stream from the plane over Hyde Park (ironically it signals an advertisement for toffee). It is also evident from the progress of the mysterious car through the streets (does it contain royalty? the Prime Minister?), and by the traditional landmarks of the city. An anonymous passer-by at St Paul's Cathedral, for instance, recognizes it as 'something which has soared beyond seeking and questing and knocking of words together and has become all spirit, disembodied, ghostly' (p. 36).

Woolf's unique understanding of this necessity to *read* the emblems in the city in order to try and make sense of it and of the characters' lives, is that the line between 'normality' and delusion is thin. Further, it is in this instance a historically determined delusion. Septimus Smith too feels that 'they are signalling to me. Not indeed in actual words; that is, he could not read the language yet; but it was plain enough, this beauty, this exquisite beauty' (p. 27). The novel therefore sheds a critical light on the social and professional mechanisms which serve to establish that line, that prevent the unreality from overwhelming the lives of those involved. For the country as a whole, it is people such as the doctor called in to treat Septimus, Sir William Bradshaw (who 'made England prosper, secluded her lunatics'), with his goddess 'Proportion', who are the chief regulators and policemen of those lives. This ideal of proportion is perceived by Bradshaw as a modern phenomenon, one 'even now engaged – in the heats and sands of India, the mud and swamp of Africa, the purlieus of London – is even now engaged in dashing down shrines, smashing idols' (p. 130).

In Sir William's eyes, therefore, the restraints of Proportion are responsible for the glories of the empire, and apply both to the imperial capital itself and to imperial 'modernizing' and 'civilizing' ambition.[11] His assurance on these matters might be questioned in the novel, though, from the presence of the traumatized colonial administrator, Peter Walsh. Yet the ironies in the novel are finally tragic; Septimus's success in committing suicide despite Bradshaw's attentions reads as a disturbance of the seeming sanctities of the social, cultural, political, and scientific assurance of London itself. These disjunctions, between internal and external 'realities', between the social fabric of the city and how it makes an impact upon the inner lives of people, marked many of the key modernist texts produced in London. Virginia Woolf here brings them to a disturbing new peak of understanding.

Dublin

Mrs Dalloway shows that Woolf had learnt something from the 'stunts' of a contemporary writer she otherwise had little time for, James Joyce. The setting of her book on a single day in the city, as well as the precise denotation of the features of buildings and of its physical spaces, leans heavily upon *Ulysses* (1922). The milieu of her novel, set amongst the affluent conservative political classes who occasionally rub shoulders with the poor only in the city's parks or through the servants in their own drawing-rooms, could, however, hardly be more remote from Joyce's. The dazzle of *Mrs Dalloway's* Bond Street, at the heart of the imperial city, is opposed to that of the colonial capital Dublin, upon which all of Joyce's novels are centred.

The historian Roy Foster has eloquently described the destitute conditions of life in Dublin in the last years of the nineteenth century and the early years of the twentieth, especially in the slums on the north side of the city's river, the Liffey. Dublin had the worst adult mortality rate in the

British Isles, and the fifth highest in the world, largely because of the 'horrific living conditions'. These conditions meant that by the outbreak of the First World War a quarter of the population were living in one-room tenements and 16,000 families were below the poverty line.[12]

Joyce's first published prose text, the collection of short stories *Dubliners* (1914), captures something of this claustrophobia and depressed hopelessness in the city. As various of the characters move through its streets, we see the deprivation through their eyes, presented without commentary by a narrator. The would-be successful poet, Little Chandler in the story 'A Little Cloud', for instance, has his sense of the entrapping misery and provincialism of his situation confirmed during a walk along Capel Street and across the Grattan Bridge:

> he looked down the river towards the quays and pitied the poor stunted houses. They seemed to him a band of tramps ... their old coats covered with dust and soot, stupefied by the panorama of sunset.[13]

After his unsatisfactory meeting with his former friend, Ignatius Gallaher, who has escaped to live in London as a journalist, Little Chandler returns home to his family (they have no servant as a cost-cutting measure, indicating the precarious social position he is in). When his baby wakes and begins to cry, so interrupting his reading of Byron, he shouts at it so loudly that the child becomes inconsolable: 'the thin walls of the room echoed the sound' (p. 74). Chandler's depressive abuse of his child is itself echoed in other of the stories. In the next story, 'Counterparts', Farrington, who has been humiliated for failing at his job, goes on a drinking spree (drinking binges by men also mark the society in these stories) and then cuts his son's thigh with a stick for having allowed the fire to go out.[14]

Repeated incidents across Joyce's stories serve to suggest the violently destructive inwardness of the domestic space in this impoverished city. Tellingly, there is sometimes a glancing suggestion that this inwardness results from Dublin's status at the time as capital of a colonized country. On Farrington's drunken progress homeward: 'His tram let him down at Shelbourne Road and he steered his great body along in the shadow of the wall of the barracks. He loathed returning to his home' (p. 82). The Beggans Bush Barracks at this time housed the occupying troops from mainland Britain. Farrington's and others' loathing and consequent violence towards the weak in *Dubliners* reflects masculine disempowerment in this historical and cultural situation, a paralysis and disablement which is exacerbated by the poor social circumstances. The book as a whole, though, ranges across class barriers, to suggest the repeated disempowerment of all in this colonial situation. 'A Painful Case', with its tale of love withheld through social con-straint, and 'The Dead', the long final story of failure in love, take place in affluent bourgeois circumstances. What they share with the otherwise socially situated stories elsewhere, however, is a sense of barriers and limits not to be crossed. Gabriel in 'The Dead', both at the New Year's party and at the end of the story when he has recognized the failure of his own love for Gretta, looks out of windows at the world beyond. Eveline, in the story bearing her name, is first encountered watching evening fall whilst sitting at the window of her house.

Joyce, in other words, reveals the agonizing sense of further possibili-ties shared by all of his characters, of further ways of living. But the repeated conclusion is that barriers, however seemingly transparent, cannot be crossed. In explaining the title of his collection in a letter, Joyce asserted that 'the expression "Dubliner" seems to me to have some meaning and I doubt whether the same could be said in such words for "Londoner" and "Parisian"'.[15] The title of the collection seems at first sight to be loose and random, but the consistent themes and imagery across the stories build towards that 'meaning', Joyce's point being that the imperial capitals of England and France could not produce this purgatorial sense of hopelessness in the same way that his stories of the colonized capital of Ireland can.

Such tetheredness of course weighs heavily upon Stephen Dedalus in Joyce's next book, *A Portrait of the Artist as a Young Man* (1916), as he conducts his own perambulations across the city, towards the moment of his famous conclusion that 'the shortest way to Tara was *via* Holyhead'. Dedalus comes to understand, in other words, that the way into the heart of Irish history (Tara is the seat of the ancient High Kings of Ireland) and consciousness is via the boat out to England and the European continent. He signals the inevitable exile of the Irish artist seeking to 'forge in the smithy of my soul the uncreated conscience of my race'.[16] As for W. B. Yeats, so for Joyce, there was a sense in which the context of colonialism had prevented the emergence of a distinct Irish identity and understanding. Both shared, though, the critical awareness that contemporary nationalist movements in Ireland were further preventing that from happening (see Chapter 5). For Joyce, however, those frustrations are to be decoded from the streets and landmarks of Dublin itself, presenting a view of modern city life which is new to literature in its directness and unmediated force of representation. *Dubliners'* 'meaning' demands an attention to particulars unfamiliar to, and resistant of, an international audience (like knowing of the Beggans Bush Barracks). In order to grasp the context for the stories, it is necessary to attend to the history of the city's situation.[17]

Paris

There is a claim to be made that modernism began to emerge in literature in the middle of the nineteenth century, with the essays and poetry of the French writer Charles Baudelaire. Baudelaire's writings on contemporary painters (particularly those on Constantin Guys and Edgar Delacroix), and the publication in 1857 of his poetry collection *Les Fleurs du mal*, established him as the foremost promoter of metropolitan modernity in literature. The influence of Baudelaire's ideas resonates across Anglo-American literary modernism, to the extent that T. S. Eliot, as late as 1930, was reappraising him as a poet who addressed the Christian concept of Original Sin: 'a greater man than was imagined, though perhaps not such a perfect poet'. Baudelaire's thinking resonates, therefore, behind Eliot's own work like *Ash-Wednesday*, published in the same year as these comments.[18]

Central to Baudelaire's concern with modernity was the issue of the relation between the artist and modern life: what he called 'the ephemeral, the fugitive, the contingent' half of art. For Baudelaire the truly modern artist is a solitary figure, 'ceaselessly journeying across the great human desert', an onlooker with respect to social customs and mores. This artist, as he suggests in the essay on Guys called 'The Painter of Modern Life', 'makes it his business to extract from fashion whatever element it may contain of poetry from history, to distil the eternal from the transitory'. In seeking to become aware of the transitory elements of modern life, the modern artist shares much with another figure whom Baudelaire perceives as having emerged in the city, the figure he famously calls a *flâneur*:

> The crowd is his element, as the air is that of birds and the water of fishes ... For the perfect *flâneur*, for the passionate spectator, it is an immense joy to set up house in the heart of the multitude, amid the ebb and flow of movement, in the midst of the fugitive and the infinite. To be away from home and yet to feel oneself everywhere at home; to see the world, to be at the centre of the world, and yet to remain hidden from the world.[19]

This sense of writer as both insider and outsider, passionate spectator of the life of the modern city, amid its ebb and flow, proved crucial for subsequent formulations of the artist's role. Through his influence upon the English poet Algernon Charles Swinburne, Baudelaire became an important figure for the Symbolist poets of the 1890s (Arthur Symons later translated his work). But the notion of the artist as ceaseless journeyer across 'the great human desert' sets him (via other French poetry also influenced by Baudelaire) as the emblematic figure behind Eliot's work from 'The Love Song of J. Alfred Prufrock' to *The Waste Land* itself. Baudelaire's 'portrait of the artist' might also be seen as agitating behind the restless modernist writers' lives, including those of Pound, H. D., Joyce, and D. H. Lawrence.

For the generation of English-language writers arriving in Paris immediately after Baudelaire's achievement, the city was already established as a central point for a consideration of the modern world. Recommending the city to a correspondent in 1867, Henry James wrote that:

> I think you will never regret having spent a large part of your time there . . . There one learns to know of men and things, and if only one gets to the point of feeling *at home* there, whatever kind of life one leads later, one will never be an ignorant person, a hermit – that is, a provincial.[20]

James's sense of the city is precisely that it challenges the cultural-backwater assumptions of America, his native land, at the time. Paris is 'universal', but also undermines narrow ideas and systems of value. 'There one learns to know of men and things'; James is already adopting the spectatorial perspective recommended by Baudelaire. As an American, he is as the modern artist should be, both inside (*at home*) and outside of the life of the city.

James's view of the exciting and unsettling but representative possibilities of Paris did not change across his long writing life. They remain themselves representative of the attitudes of those later writers who moved to the city seeking freedoms of various kinds – sexual, political, and social. These included fellow American compatriots Gertrude Stein, F. Scott Fitzgerald, Ernest Hemingway, Ezra Pound, Djuna Barnes, and the Irishman James Joyce amongst them. James's 1903 novel *The Ambassadors* captures these tensions perfectly. Lambert Strether is sent from Massachusetts to Paris in order to bring back the son of Mrs Newsome, with whom Strether has an intimate if ambiguous relationship. Chad Newsome is rumoured to have been corrupted by the various licences that Paris offers, even to have become attached to a woman there, and so is in danger of losing his inheritance through failing to take over his father's business back home. As Strether arrives in Europe, his middle-aged sense of purpose and of the moral correctness of the journey immediately starts to be diffused, however. On arrival at his staging-post in England, he feels 'a consciousness of personal freedom as he hadn't known for years'. Once he gets to Paris, this feeling accelerates, as he becomes embroiled in his own different relationships to the eventual abandonment of his project:

Poor Strether had at this very moment to recognize the truth that wherever one paused in Paris the imagination reacted before one could stop it. This perpetual reaction put a price, if one would, on pauses; but it piled up consequences till there was scarce room to pick one's steps among them.[21]

Strether, like James, was alert to the tawdriness and superficiality of Paris and of the salon society found there. Yet, at the same time, *The Ambassadors* rapidly ceases to focus on Chad Newsome, who appears in contrast as a rather conventional figure, and concentrates instead upon the growth into 'personal freedom' which Strether experiences.

It is those qualities of the city which rapidly led to other American writers settling there. Gertrude Stein arrived in Paris in 1903. Her arrival soon put her in touch with the group of visual artists which the British public was only to become aware of through Roger Fry's Post-Impressionist exhibitions of 1910 and 1912, and the majority of American art-lovers through the Armory show of 1913. Stein's friendship with the French painter Henri Matisse, and more especially that with the Spaniard Pablo Picasso, as well as her early acquaintance with the work of Paul Cézanne, had immediate effects upon her own writing's crucial move towards modernism. Stein's triptych of portraits, *Three Lives* (1909), bears the mark of these influences, particularly in its descriptive passages, where the human form tends towards abstraction, as it does in the work of these artists:

Mrs Haydon was all a compact and well hardened mass, even to her face, reddish and darkened from its early blonde, with its hearty, shiny, cheeks, and doubled chin well covered over with the uproll of her short, square neck.

The two daughters, who were fourteen and fifteen, looked like unkneaded, unformed mounds of flesh beside her.[22]

This is a writing that is interested in form and colour, and which reads character through appearance. It is also interested in analysing the juxtaposition between shapes, and in presenting the visual image directly and without commentary. The development of this technique in Stein's writing was something she later related to her daily involvement with Picasso at the time when his painting was moving towards its modernist phase with the abstract rearrangement of form that was Cubism. Stein, upon her arrival in Paris, had soon established a Saturday-evening salon which attracted the major poets (including Guillaume Apollinaire) and painters of the time. Picasso was an early and regular attender. *Three Lives* was partly composed by Stein during her numerous sittings for the portrait of her finished by

Picasso in 1906. The portrait shows Stein's own massive body topped by a primitive, mask-like head, the kind of head that was soon to become familiar through Picasso's brothel-set Cubist masterpiece of 1907, *Les Demoiselles d'Avignon*.

Cubism, as it was developed by Picasso with his friend Georges Braque, attacked traditional perspective in painting (as Stein does in writing), bringing the subject of the work towards the plane of the picture surface. It also attacked traditional notions of figural realism in art, whereby we *assume* that a body painted on the surface of a canvas has a depth and three-dimensional reality. Picasso and Braque dissect the figure in their Cubist work, and present different views of it simultaneously. To this extent, their work is abstract rather than representational. It takes juxtaposed forms and masses and sets them alongside each other on the canvas, as we can see Stein doing in the description above from 'The Gentle Lena'. Such juxtaposition was to become technically important for later American works influenced by Cubism, such as the poet Wallace Stevens's 'Thirteen Ways of Looking at a Blackbird'.[23] This move away from representation was, notoriously, partly sparked by the interest of painters like Picasso and Matisse in African sculpture. Typically, however, Stein, in her later displaced 1933 autobiography, which appeared as *The Autobiography of Alice B. Toklas* (Toklas was her long-term companion and lover), asserted the importance of her own role in the new movement:

> In those early days when [Picasso] created cubism the effect of the african art was purely upon his vision and his forms, his imagination remained purely spanish. The spanish quality of ritual and abstraction had indeed been stimulated by his painting of the portrait of Gertrude Stein. She had a definite impulse then and always toward elemental abstraction.[24]

Whatever the 'truth' or otherwise of this influence, the style of this shows the continuing impact of modernist visual art upon Stein's writing. Each sentence stands at an oblique angle to the ones preceding and following it, and offers a new start or 'take' on the subject from a different perspective. The whole approach of the *Autobiography*, in which Stein narrates her experiences of Paris through the 'voice' of her lover, is of course a furtherance of this technique. Stein is seen from the 'outside', and her opinions and actions are perceived as if not her own. The Paris milieu, then, provided Stein with a significant impulse towards a new and different kind of writing, one which was in its turn to have an impact upon the writing of those subsequently drawn into her coterie – writers including Ernest Hemingway and (to a lesser extent), F. Scott Fitzgerald.

New York

The event that saw the beginnings of a specifically American modernism, although one highly dependent upon the European ideas and personalities mentioned above, was the 1913 Armory show of the visual arts held in New York. The show introduced the broader American public to modern European painting, much as the two London Post-Impressionist exhibitions had done in the preceding years. And, just as in London, the painting of the Post-Impressionists and Cubists had an impact upon an emerging native and self-consciously modern literature. At the centre of the Armory show was a painting of 1912 by Marcel Duchamp, 'Nude Descending a Staircase No. 2'. When Duchamp himself arrived in New York in 1915, in flight from the First World War, a salon of poets and painters including Man Ray, Wallace Stevens, and William Carlos Williams gathered around him at the apartment of the wealthy art patron Walter Arensberg. In the same year, the magazine *Others* appeared, financed by Arensberg, and members of the group went on to launch the First Annual Exhibition of the Society of Independent Artists in April 1917. It was the exclusion of Duchamp's so-called 'ready-made' work, consisting of a porcelain urinal on top of a pedestal entitled 'Fountain by R. Mutt', from this exhibition which notoriously launched a debate about the nature and purpose of art. This was a debate which resonated across American visual art across the first half of the twentieth century, down to Jackson Pollock's 'action paintings' and the movement of Abstract Expressionism in the late 1940s.

In literature, the impact of such visual innovation was immediate. The poet Wallace Stevens, in his first collection *Harmonium* (1923), developed a hieratic and dandified rhetoric that challenges the reader's response. Several of the poems ('Domination of Black', 'Last Looks at the Lilacs', 'Of the Surface of Things', amongst others) draw attention to their genesis in perception. More specifically, the playful attitude towards subject matter displayed throughout the book owes something to the controversy surrounding Duchamp's ready-mades, in the sense that material is happened upon rather than deliberately sought out. Most famously, the typical poem 'Anecdote of the Jar', in which the poet imagines placing a jar in the Tennessee wilderness, suggests the ways in which banal and mundane materials can provide perspective and meaning upon untamed space. By putting the jar in the landscape, the speaker brings focus and civilized possibilities to the wild provincial sprawl of Tennessee. But the jar itself, whatever its proclaimed achievement from this perspective, remains unchanged and insignificant: 'It took dominion everywhere. / The jar was gray and bare.'[25] Stevens's work, here as throughout his career, delights in the random yet transformational and symbolic achievements of such concatenations.

The movement towards a specifically American avant-garde in the wake of the New York Armory show in the latter part of the 1910s was mirrored in less precious and more democratic terms over the next few years by the cultural 'Renaissance' occurring in another district of New York – Harlem. By 1925, looking back over the past decade, James Weldon Johnson felt enabled to announce that Harlem had become 'The Culture Capital'. He boldly suggested that the new centre of American artistic activity was to be found in the district of Manhattan which, across the past forty years, had seen a major influx of African Americans from the south and the Caribbean. A group of writers that included poets Langston Hughes and Claude McKay, prose writers Jean Toomer, Rudolph Fisher and Zora Neale Hurston, and a gathering of black academics and cultural commentators, were ambitiously generating and proclaiming from within the Harlem artistic community an innovatory energy. That energy might be taken to parallel and to interfuse with modern technical tendencies elsewhere.

In one of the articles which he contributed to the key contemporary gathering of texts from what came to be called the Harlem Renaissance, *The New Negro* (which he also edited), the philosopher, polemicist and academic Alain Locke noted amongst its writers

> the increasing tendency to evolve from the racial substance something technically distinctive, something that as an idiom of style may become a contribution to the general resources of art . . . In music such transfusions of racial idioms with the modernistic styles of expression have already taken place; in the other arts it is just as possible and likely . . . Toomer gives a musical folk-lilt and a glamorous sensuous ecstasy to the style of the American prose modernists.[26]

Locke's focus is a dual one both here and elsewhere in *The New Negro* anthology. He looks towards the emergent literature of the 'new Negro' in Harlem, and beyond to the new artistic movements in America and Europe. In the title essay he discusses the recent 'spiritual emancipation' of the African American population in the metropolis, 'this renewed self-respect and self-dependence' brought about by the ending of slavery in the mid-nineteenth century and the migration to the northern cities at the start of the twentieth. There has arisen, he notes, a new modernity and a new flourishing of poetry, drama, music, and the visual arts from young black artists. This might in turn form part of a movement which is elsewhere leading art, specifically European art, away from what he calls elsewhere its 'decadence and sterility' (pp. 258–62). Ethnic and African art, as several contributors to *The New Negro* perceive, have recently re-inflected the visual arts for artists across a range of nationalities and backgrounds, from the Spanish/French artist Picasso to the Jewish-American artist Jacob Epstein. 'Racial' and 'folk-lilt' rhythms have also entered modernist music in works by the French composers Eric Satie and Darius Milhaud and in the ballet scores of the Russian Igor Stravinsky. Harlem, Locke concludes, has the 'same role to play for the New Negro as Dublin has had for the New Ireland' – Ireland having finally received its partial independence from Britain in 1922 (p. 7).

The Harlem Renaissance claimed, therefore, a joyful sense of independence from former oppression, whilst at the same time signalling the rightful place of the 'new Negro' and of Harlem artists alongside other modern American writers seeking to define the new nation as a whole. In a poem included by Locke, Langston Hughes's 'I Too', the poet offers a challenge to the 'singing' celebration of America by its original white poetic celebrant, Walt Whitman. In direct response to works such as Whitman's 'inscription' 'I Hear America Singing', which conceives of the nation as a union of happy workers and tradespeople, Hughes adopts the persona of a black house servant who is relegated to the kitchen when guests arrive. This servant, however, can imagine a new dawning since 'I, too, sing America' and can imagine the day when 'they'll see how beautiful I am' (p. 145).

What remains distinctive about this writing is its occasional tapping of folk elements ('the unique spiritual products of American life', as Locke himself calls them in his essay on 'The Negro Spirituals'), as well as the inclusion of intonations of dialect speech (p. 199).[27] This is further the case when the writing adopts the intonations and rhythms of jazz, a musical idiom 'one part American and three parts American Negro' as J. A. Rogers maintains, although a craze now appropriated by sophisticates in Paris and London (p. 216). Rogers's piece essentializes the qualities of jazz as a 'Negro rhythm' particularly to be found in the lower classes in Harlem, and it is this rhythm which is captured by the title poem of Langston Hughes's 1926 collection *The Weary Blues*, in which we see a player on an old piano, sitting on a rickety stool, but expressing 'a black man's soul':

> Droning a drowsy syncopated tune,
> Rocking back and forth to a mellow croon,
>   I heard a Negro play.
> Down on Lenox Avenue the other night
> By the pale dull pallor of an old gas light
>   He did a lazy sway . . .
>   He did a lazy sway . . .

The poem remains a song of protest, in that the blues sung are 'weary' due to the singer's dissatisfaction with his situation to the extent that he would rather be dead. And yet the syncopation of the poem's own rhythms captures further possibilities in the city through its celebration of an integration between voice, protest, and music ('Ain't got nobody in all this world, / Ain't go nobody but ma self').[28]

It is this jazz element of the Harlem Renaissance which perhaps suggested to white writers the most potential for cross-over into a new kind of writing. Jazz, of course, resonates through the novels of F. Scott Fitzgerald, but appears also as a formal possibility in more unlikely places. Richard Aldington, the original English Imagist poet who was also a novelist and editor, for instance, surprisingly described the technique of his novel partly drawing upon his own experience in the trenches of the First World War, *Death of a Hero* (1929), as 'jazz'. The poet Mina Loy, herself aware of her 'mongrel' condition as an Anglo-Jewish writer who became the doyenne of American poetry circles in the late 1910s, wrote her only manifesto on 'Modern Poetry' in about 1925. Loy contentiously claims there that 'the new poetry of the English language has proceeded out of America', that it stands alongside 'American jazz' in its potential, and seems partly inflected by these new musical rhythms. Loy's reason for this acclamation depends upon her sense of the linguistic hybridity of the English language in America, 'where latterly a thousand languages have been born'. This hybridity is especially audible, she argues, in the New York streets: 'The composite language is a very living language, it grows as you speak ... on the baser avenues of Manhattan every voice swings to the triple rhythm of its race, its citizenship and its personality.'[29]

Her 1927 poem, 'The Widow's Jazz', on her gone-missing husband Arthur Cravan, is but the most obvious of her works in which the syncopated rhythm and savoured vowel sounds sustain a complex interweaving of cultural and personal allusion (p. 96):

> Cravan
> colossal absentee
> the substitute dark
> rolls to the incandescent memory
>
> of love's survivor
> on this rich suttee
>
> seared by the flames of sound
> the widowed urn
>
> holds impotently
> your murdered laughter

This establishes a jazz rhythm between its sub-sections through its use of assonance and rhyme (absentee/memory/impotently, survivor/laughter) and complex alliteration. Despite the wall of segregation between the races in Harlem itself, therefore, the work to establish a cultural renewal adequate to the newly metropolitan America allowed for cultural cross-fertilization on the New York streets. That modernist interest in 'primitive' images and energies, which in Europe could smack of cultural fetishism, in America released new energies and vocal possibilities for a range of native and émigré writers.

Non- and anti-metropolitan modernisms

There is a strain in modernism which resists the cosmopolitan and Europe-influenced celebrations of the modern metropolis, be it New York, London, or Paris. The racial and dialect voice, which emerges sometimes to distinguish the distinctive energies of the Harlem Renaissance, finds equivalence in sometimes opposed political and social identifications elsewhere at this time. The novels set in the southern United States by William Faulkner, including *As I Lay Dying* (1930), utilize, for instance, a disjunctive local dialect voice alongside a formal dependence upon traditional craftsmanship. Modernism, in other words, continued to draw upon local and regional inflections outside of the hybridized voices of the city, as well as being fascinated by the possible mixings and mingling on the city streets. These two 'pulls' upon the literary voice often cross each other in interesting ways.

At the time that he was writing his classically informed Imagist work, for instance, the most cosmopolitan of the moderns Ezra Pound was writing admiringly of the work scored for the regional voices of the American New England poet Robert Frost and the English Nottinghamshire poet and novelist D. H. Lawrence. Whilst distancing himself from the formal conventionality of both, Pound admires their similar traits of directness. 'Mr Frost is an honest writer, writing from himself', he declares, and has 'dared to write . . . in the natural speech of New England'. 'This man has the good sense to speak naturally.' When quoting Lawrence's poems in Midlands dialect, Pound again admires the fact that 'the characters are real . . . Mr Lawrence has attempted realism and attained it.'[30] Pound's imitations of Yankee, accented English, and adoptions of Negro blackface punctuate his epic *The Cantos*. At this level, the modernist project draws upon those refusals of internationally standardized English that have ambitions wholly other than Pound and Eliot's preoccupation with what the latter called 'the mind of Europe'. In a curious counter-movement, Pound (and the Eliot of the

Cockney speech in the pub scene in *The Waste Land*) enjoys the pace and vibrancy of spontaneous, non-literary idiom, and often also one related to a specific sense of place. It is this resistance to the cosmopolitan, internationalist aspects of modernism I wish to discuss in this chapter's final section. Despite their politicized refusal of certain dominant aspects of writing in this period, writers such as Frost and Lawrence, after all, experienced not dissimilar feelings of unsettledness with regard to their relation to the past and their world to those of the metropolitan coteries.

Frost's 'North of Boston' is a place in which he seeks to found a native American poetics upon the necessity to clear the New World's land for a new social and cultural possibility. The dubiously colonial nature of this personal, but also national, ambition is evident from an early sonnet like 'Mowing', from Frost's 1913 first collection *A Boy's Will*:

> There was never a sound beside the wood but one,
> And that was my long scythe whispering to the ground.
> What was it it whispered? I knew not well myself . . .

Frost's straightforward celebration of seasonal rituals upon the land ('The fact is the sweetest dream that labor knows') presents itself here as a transient stage before the completion of an original kind of art. The mowing 'left the hay to make', but at least prepares the way for that achievement.[31] The modernity of Frost's project lies, however, in his paradoxically assured uncertainties and self-qualifications, his sense that the project, as here, might be failing to catch or to understand correctly the true nature and possibilities of the situation ('What was it it whispered? I knew not well . . .'). Across his early collections of the 1910s and into the 1920s, Frost explored both the overwhelming abundance of his New England pastoral and its uncertain metaphysics.

In 'After Apple-Picking', the dynamic between the harvest of the land's good fruits and larger prospects is established as 'I am drowsing off . . . For I have had too much / Of apple-picking: I am overtired / Of the great harvest I myself desired.' The speaker's anxiety, resonant with Christian notions of grace, is that he not 'let fall' any of the 'ten thousand thousand fruit' which have got into his dreams. But the end of the poem again opens out, rather than resolves, the strenuous perplexities of the situation. Frost cannot be certain of his mastery over his relation to the harvest or, therefore, of its implied cultural, territorial, and poetic significance. It is not for the poet, he concludes as he falls asleep, to establish whether he has come into harmony with these broader possibilities. Rather, it is for forces like the native fauna outside of him, which are silent or absent, to provide the ratification which he requires (p. 71):

> Were he not gone,
> The woodchuck could say whether it's like his
> Long sleep, as I describe its coming on,
> Or just some human sleep.

The speaker's situation in this local landscape is uncertain and excessive, despite the delight he takes in its new fertility and the poetry that comes from it. He cannot be certain that the sleep induced by his labour on the land forms a kind of hibernation which will lead to a new dawning in a new American spring, or whether it is simply an autumnal exhaustion and jadedness which will lead on into the darkness of winter. For all of his hope in the new pastoral, therefore, Frost's work remains dubious of its gift and destiny. The alternative perspective offered upon experience by this determinedly local voice shares something of the disturbance to be discovered in the declaredly modern writing of those contemporaries in the cities or other new historical circumstances.

A similar unsettledness marks the relation of English writers at the time to non-urban spaces. A key impetus to Frost's career, indeed, had come from the time he spent in England in 1912–14, where he met pastoral English poets, including most notably Edward Thomas. This unsettledness is true not only of those poets, like Thomas, who found themselves writing in the trenches of the Western Front in the First World War (see the discussion in the next chapter), but it is true also of those writers, both those interested in dialect or otherwise, who continued to draw upon versions of pastoral within their more concertedly modern focus. D. H. Lawrence's late autobiographical essay 'Nottingham and the Mining Countryside' captures this essential ambivalence when recalling the group of houses called the 'Breach' in Eastwood. These were houses, owned by the mining company his father worked for, in one of which he lived as a boy:

> We lived in the Breach, in a corner house. A field-path came down under a great hawthorn hedge. On the other side was the brook, with the old sheep-bridge going over into the meadows ... So that the life was a curious cross between industrialism and the old agricultural England of Shakespeare and Milton and Fielding and George Eliot. The dialect was broad Derbyshire, and always 'thee' and 'thou'.

His sense of this liminal, on-the-edge condition, leads Lawrence to argue that England has never developed 'the real *urban* side of man, the civic side'. Therefore, the attempt of the English to achieve a modern space for post-industrial life has led to 'the real tragedy of England ... the tragedy of ugliness. The country is so lovely: the man-made England is so vile.'[32]

Lawrence draws upon nineteenth-century English writing, including that of John Ruskin and William Morris, to castigate that loss of beauty. He laments the lost link with the country which he felt had continued down to the generation of his miner father, who picked mushrooms and chased rabbits on his daily walk across the fields to his work at Brinsley pit.

Lawrence's early novels, from *The White Peacock* (1911) through *Sons and Lovers* (1913) to *The Rainbow* (1915), all explore this between-time and between-spaces sense of his historical situation in England. The romance between Paul Morel and Miriam Leivers in *Sons and Lovers* is precisely mapped onto the local landscape around Eastwood ('Bestwood' in the book). The journeys by Paul out of the mining town to the Leivers' farm provide the shift from the realm of family claustrophobia, violence, and constriction for the budding artist towards a world of possibility. In the final pages of the novel, however, this sense of the liminal space operates in reverse, reflecting the ambivalence in which it is held for Lawrence. After the failure of his relationship with Miriam and of another with Clara Dawes, Paul stands on the edge of the town brooding upon the loss also of his beloved mother:

> He could not bear it. On every side the immense dark silence seemed pressing him, so tiny a speck, into extinction, and yet, almost nothing, he could not be extinct ... no, he could not give in. Turning sharply, he walked towards the city's gold phosphorescence ... He would not take that direction, to the darkness, to follow her.[33]

The country here is an ahistorical space, just as it has been across the novel in its relation to the figure of the otherworldly Miriam. Paul's move back towards the city is an acceptance of the need to wrestle with the present, in all of its 'ugliness'.

A similar situation arises at the end of Lawrence's next published novel, *The Rainbow*. The most outward-looking of the modern generation of the Brangwen family, Ursula, ends the novel with hope, having recovered from illness after a miscarriage following her split from her lover Anton Skrebensky:

> She saw the stiffened bodies of the colliers, which seemed already enclosed in a coffin, she saw their unchanging eyes, the eyes of those who are buried alive ... she saw the dun atmosphere over the blackened hills opposite, the dark blotches of houses, slate roofed and amorphous ... and she was sick with a nausea so deep that she perished as she sat. And then, in the blowing clouds, she saw a band of faint iridescence colouring in faint colours a portion of the hill.[34]

The advent of the rainbow, both natural phenomenon here and retrieved biblical sign of the covenant between God and man, marks a symbol of Ursula's faith in the 'new germination' of human possibility, as she looks back from the countryside to the mining hill-town in which she lives.[35] It is an apocalyptic vision, in that it foresees the sweeping away of humankind and its replacement by a new form of living. These last pages of the novel are overwritten by Lawrence's final revisions of the book in late 1914 and the first half of 1915, as it became clear that the conflict in Europe in the trenches of World War One was to cause massive slaughter on both sides. The closing vision of the 'indomitable' arch of the rainbow in these paragraphs derives, then, from Lawrence's double perspective, sustained across his career, between the traditions of the country and the imposed conditions of the industrial town. He is caught between a perspective outside of history and one vitally alert to the forces of historical cataclysm all around.

A similar doubling of perspective persists in English novels written both before and after Lawrence's. E. M. Forster's *Howards End* (1910) exhibits the strain between the old country house of the title which imbues the nature of its owner, Mrs Wilcox, and the world of modern capitalism in the city of London. When we first see Mrs Wilcox, walking noiselessly around the house, 'she seemed to belong . . . to the house, and to the tree that over-shadowed it . . . she worshipped the past, and . . . the instinctive wisdom the past can alone bestow had descended upon her'. In this, Margaret Schlegel, to whom she gives the house in her will, a fact hidden from Margaret by the imperial capitalist Wilcoxes, shares her vision.[36] Henry Wilcox's business is the Imperial and West African Rubber Company; imperialism, we are told, 'had always been one of [Margaret's] difficulties' (p. 197).

This is a consciously pre-war novel. Margaret is aware that the headlines in the popular press like 'England and Germany are bound to fight' will only make war more inevitable (p. 74). But she is principally preoccupied by the 'chaotic nature of our daily life' (p. 115). Of Margaret in the capital city, we learn, 'London thwarted her; in its atmosphere she could not concentrate. London only stimulates, it cannot sustain' (p. 155). London, in other words, to her mind prevents those connections between people and across history which the novel idealistically seeks to realize, and which Howards End itself symbolizes. Margaret never gets to occupy her inheritance, however. Her marriage to Henry Wilcox, partly made to keep that inheritance secret, paradoxically prevents her coming into her true place. Forster's irony throughout, of course, is that it is Margaret Schlegel, the daughter of a German idealist father, who is the natural heir to this most English of retreats. For Forster, as for Lawrence and other writers of the time including

Ford Madox Ford, the pressures of modern industry, international finance, and empire are breaking traditional relationships with the extra-urban fastness of England. At the start of Chapter XIX in the novel, the narrator seeks to find a perspective from which 'to show a foreigner England', and settles upon the Purbeck hills near Corfe. But he cannot rest in this pastoral vision without having to acknowledge that impinging upon it are 'red houses, and the Stock Exchange' (p. 170). The growing commuter belt, which even at this time Forster takes as having extended to the 'ignoble coast' near Bournemouth, threatens a true relationship with the country, and crowds upon perspectives across the landscape.

As also for Lawrence, so for Virginia Woolf, it is the historical break caused by the First World War which further exacerbates such disconnection. In the first part of *To the Lighthouse* (1927), Woolf establishes 'the lost garden' of the Ramsay family's holiday home in Skye as a place of seemingly extra-historical potential, the setting for a late Victorian world which might have gone on forever. The parents, as seen by the painter Lily Briscoe, on the lawn of the house come to seem 'symbolical': 'So that is marriage, Lily thought, a man and a woman looking at a girl throwing a ball. That is what Mrs Ramsay tried to tell me the other night, she thought.'[37] But history, in the shape of war, rudely interrupts this potentially idyllic and meaningful setting, with the narrative- and rapid time-shift brought about in the bracketed brief central section of the book 'Time Passes'.

History is both remote to the continued setting, which remains focused upon the holiday house, but also devastates it, as first a Ramsay daughter dies in childbirth, then a son at the Front, then Mrs Ramsay herself dies. The final section of the novel finds the key figures back at the house, but Lily Briscoe is now left seeking to recover in her painting that harmony and centredness which has vanished in actuality from the scene with the death of Mrs Ramsay. It is only when she can recover a 'vision' of Mrs Ramsay, sitting on the steps of the house knitting, that 'the problem might be solved after all', as it is when she puts a line down the centre of her canvas at the place in her picture from which the older woman has vanished (pp. 218, 226). As with Woolf's and others' writing about the city, it is the subjective which triumphs over the actual here.

Woolf, like Lawrence and Forster, finds in the non-urban places of England a ghostly presence of earlier 'meaning' and possibility. But it is a meaning which is always under threat from forces within the present – forces that interrupt and disrupt the tradition, at the same time as it is sought after in an attempt through art to rediscover what it is that history has managed to wreck. With World War One this process would accelerate, bringing new challenges for emergent modernist writing.

Notes

1 The drift to the towns in the latter part of the nineteenth century and into the early twentieth extended across Britain, but, by 1911, nearly 20 per cent of the nation's population lived in London. See Jose Harris, *Private Lives, Public Spirit: Britain 1870–1914* (Harmondsworth, 1994), p. 42. In Ireland, there was a similar influx to Dublin, across these years, due to agricultural crises in the late nineteenth century. See Roy Foster, *Modern Ireland 1600–1972* (Harmondsworth, 1989), pp. 436–7.

2 Robert Louis Stevenson, *Dr Jekyll and Mr Hyde and Other Stories*, edited by Jenni Calder (Harmondsworth, 1979), p. 48.

3 The social mobility of the rising middle classes was a noted feature of British cultural and professional life from the 1880s onwards. See Eric Hobsbawm, *The Age of Empire 1875–1914* (London, 1987), pp. 172–3.

4 George Gissing, *New Grub Street*, edited by John Goode (Oxford, 1993), p. 106.

5 Ezra Pound was the 'foreign correspondent' in London for the Chicago-based *Poetry* from 1912 to 1917, and did much to introduce the emerging generation of modernist poets, including T. S. Eliot, to the American audience. From 1917 to 1919 he was the 'foreign editor' for New York's *The Little Review*, during which time the editors were prosecuted for their publication of sections of James Joyce's *Ulysses*. *The Egoist* in London also serialized portions of Joyce's novel as well as of Wyndham Lewis's *Tarr*. It included on its editorial staff the English poet and novelist Richard Aldington and the American poet H. D. (1914–17), before being edited by T. S. Eliot from 1917. Eliot went on to edit his own journal, *The Criterion*, whose first number included his *The Waste Land* (1922). Later, the American poet Marianne Moore edited *The Dial* (1925–9), and did much to promote the later developments of modernism. Greater modernist control of the means of literary production than this was exerted by Virginia Woolf, when she went into business with Leonard Woolf to found the Hogarth Press. The Press brought out her own writings as well as other important modernist texts by women, including works by Katherine Mansfield and Gertrude Stein.

6 Arthur Symons, *Cities* (London, 1903), p. v.

7 Ford Madox Ford, *The Soul of London*, edited by Alan G. Hill (London, 1995), pp. 4, 9, 15, 16.

8 Joseph Conrad, *The Secret Agent* (Harmondsworth, 1980), pp. 138–9.

9 Virginia Woolf, *Mrs Dalloway*, edited by Claire Tomalin (Oxford, 1992), p. 13.

10 The passage also shows the important impact upon Woolf, as upon the other modernists, of the ideas of the French philosopher Henri Bergson. Bergson famously described two versions of time – mechanical time (the hours as they pass), and our inner understanding of that mechanical duration. 'We perceive the physical world and this perception appears, rightly or wrongly, to be inside and outside us at one and the same time; in one way, it is a state of consciousness; in another, a surface film of matter in which perceiver and perceived coincide. To each moment of our inner life there thus corresponds a moment of our body and of all environing matter that is "simultaneous" with it.' See *Henri Bergson: Key Writings*, edited by Keith Ansell Pearson and John Mullarkey (London, 2002), p. 205.

11 See Elleke Boehmer, *Colonial and Postcolonial Literature: Migrant Metaphors* (Oxford, 1995), pp. 142–3.

12 Foster, *Modern Ireland*, pp. 142–3.

13 James Joyce, *The Essential James Joyce*, edited by Harry Levin (Frogmore, 1977), p. 65.

14 The National Society for the Prevention of Cruelty to Children noted in a report that, just after the turn of the century, there was a comparatively low level of drunkenness in Dublin compared with other Irish cities such as Cork and Belfast. But, on the other hand, they were 'emphatic' that drunkenness was the main factor in the cases they handled there. See Mary E. Daly, *Dublin: The Deposed Capital. A Social and Economic History 1860–1914* (Cork, 1984), pp. 81–2.

15 *Selected Letters of James Joyce*, edited by Richard Ellmann (London, 1992), p. 79.

16 James Joyce, *A Portrait of the Artist as a Young Man*, edited by Seamus Deane (Harmondsworth, 1992), pp. 273, 276.

17 This translation of Joyce's specific insight into a template for the methodologies of international modernism of course began more or less immediately, with the response by T. S. Eliot to *Ulysses*. Eliot's essay, '*Ulysses*, Order and Myth' (1923), with its famous celebration of Joyce's technique in the novel, and its adumbration of a 'mythical method' as a means of controlling the futility of contemporary history, suggested the readiness for appropriation and abstraction underlying modernism's versions of itself. Eliot's version of the shattered imperial capital, London, in the aftermath of the First World War in *The Waste Land*, might owe much to Joyce's vision and technique in anatomizing the colonial city, Dublin. But in the gap between the two texts another history and politics has been leached away.

18 T. S. Eliot, *Selected Essays* (London, 1972), p. 420.

19 Charles Baudelaire, *The Painter of Modern Life and Other Essays*, translated by Jonathan Mayne (London, 1964), pp. 10, 9, 12.

20 Henry James, *A Life in Letters*, edited by Philip Horne (Harmondsworth, 1999), p. 14.

21 Henry James, *The Ambassadors*, edited by Philip Hensher (Harmondsworth, 2001), pp. 3, 64.

22 Gertrude Stein, *Three Lives* (New York, 1990), p. 174.

23 See John Richardson, 'The Coming of Cubism', in *A Life of Picasso, 1907–1917: The Painter of Modern Life* (London, 1996), pp. 101–21.

24 Gertrude Stein, *The Autobiography of Alice B. Toklas* (Harmondsworth, 2001), pp. 71–2.

25 Wallace Stevens, *Collected Poems* (London, 1984), p. 76.

26 'Negro Youth Speaks', in *The New Negro*, edited by Alain Locke (New York, 1925; 1992 edition), p. 50. W. E. B. Dubois's achievement in his collection of stories about African Americans in *The Souls of Black Folk* (1903) clearly does something to underwrite the confidence of later activists like Locke.

27 Michael North has noted that several of the leading white American modernists, and most significantly Ezra Pound and T. S. Eliot, adopted blackface and pretended to be African Americans in their letters and privately circulated poems. This, he argues, was a strategy to keep their own language resources alive against contemporary movements seeking to standardize English. Black 'dialect' became for them, North concludes, 'the private double of the modernist poetry they were jointly creating' at the time in London. *The Dialect of Modernism: Race, Language and Twentieth-Century Literature* (New York, 1994), p. 77.

28 Langston Hughes, *Selected Poems* (London, 1999), p. 33.

29 Mina Loy, 'Modern Poetry', in *The Lost Lunar Baedecker*, selected and edited by Roger Conover (New York, 1996), pp. 157, 159.

30 Ezra Pound, 'Robert Frost (Two Reviews)' and 'D. H. Lawrence', in *Literary Essays of Ezra Pound*, edited by T. S. Eliot (London, 1954), pp. 382–4, 388.

31 Robert Frost, 'Mowing', in *Collected Poems, Prose, and Plays*, edited by Richard Poirier and Mark Richardson (New York, 1995), p. 26.

32 D. H. Lawrence, 'Nottingham and the Mining Countryside', in *Phoenix: The Posthumous Papers of D. H. Lawrence*, edited by Edward D. McDonald (London, 1967), pp. 135, 137.

33 D. H. Lawrence, *Sons and Lovers*, edited by Helen Baron and Carl Baron (Harmondsworth, 1994), p. 464.

34 D. H. Lawrence, *The Rainbow*, edited by John Worthen (Harmondsworth, 1989), pp. 547–8.

35 This perspective, at least, is suggested by the pen-and-wash drawing which Lawrence gave to Viola Meynell on completion of his novel, 2 March 1915. In the drawing, sheaves of wheat stand in the foreground, and the rainbow stands over a colliery in the middle distance in front of the town.

36 E. M. Forster, *Howards End*, edited by Oliver Stallybrass (Harmondsworth, 2000), p. 36.

37 Virginia Woolf, *To the Lighthouse* (Harmondsworth, 1992), pp. 79–80.

|3|

Modernist wars and conflicts

The period of World War One, which took place between August 1914 and November 1918, instigated radical changes in the form and content of literary texts in English. For American émigrés in London across the time of the conflict, including Pound and Eliot, the war brought confirmation, if also a re-inflection, of the innovative literary techniques they had been experimenting with in the previous five or six years. But it also, as we shall see, significantly reoriented their subject matter. During and after the war, they moved away from the concerns with aestheticism and society which marked their earlier work. They now sought literary parallels for the current situation, and conducted an investigation into the nature of that 'civiliza-tion' which the war was purportedly fought to preserve. For emerging English novelists at the time, including D. H. Lawrence and Virginia Woolf, meditation upon the catastrophe brought the requirement of stylistic and formal change in their work – change that would reflect the alteration in the psyche of the nation caused by the conflict.

As Extract 2 (pp. 141–2) from an article in *The New Age* (a magazine devoted to economics and literature) reveals, these issues were resonating from the early months of the conflict. In considering the commonly held belief at the time that it was the militaristic tradition of the dominant sub-culture in Germany, that of the Prussians, which was responsible for war, C. Grant Robertson is patriotically forced to review the values upon which Britain, and the British Empire, have stood. Key to that review are terms like 'civilization' (as opposed to the 'barbarism' imputed to those who did not display such values) and 'our heritage': the set of 'principles' that ensure the continuation of freedom and of the British state itself. Few writers under consideration in this book would be as unguarded or relatively unsophisti-cated as Robertson is here, but his words are helpful in considering the atmosphere under which all of these writers, both British and American, lived during the war. For this was a time of tension both from without and within, and, if these writers' response to the devastating battles was more nuanced than Robertson's, their presumptions, about coherence and the 'organic whole' of traditional political and social life in Britain, were often not dissimilar to his.

Many earlier presumptions, including those about national inviolability, the location of culture, and the nature of relations between the sexes, came under scrutiny across these years. More specifically, fears about cultural degeneration, which had haunted European life since the 1890s (and which had been encapsulated in the 1895 book *Degeneration* by Max Nordau), became exacerbated by a variety of issues. The war revived doubts about the imperial enterprise, which had grown with the British hard-won victory in the Anglo-Boer War of 1899–1902. The earlier conflict had in its turn brought the British nation's attention to bear upon the sharp internal social and class divisions, which continued to lack redress even under the reforms introduced by the Liberal administration from 1906. Forty per cent of those recruited to serve in South Africa were rejected as physically unfit, exposing the effects of poverty, poor diet, and housing upon the rising urban labouring class. In spite of a 1904 Interdepartmental Report into Physical Deterioration, over 50 per cent of recruits were still being rejected on these grounds in 1910. A high figure of rejections (including one for D. H. Lawrence) hampered the numbers raised through compulsory conscription into the forces, which arrived in the middle of the war: 1914–18 therefore raised further doubts about issues of social policy, gender, sexual difference, and the masculinity which had been held across the Victorian era to be the basis upon which the empire rested. Such doubts were strengthened with the return of the maimed, wounded, and shell-shocked from the Western Front. All of these issues are reflected in the texts which were written immediately in response to the European crisis, and in those that later reflected upon it. This chapter will review some of the forces, uncertainties, and traumas reflected in literature at this time of seemingly accelerated historical change.

The war arrived after years of appearing to be about to break out, through the many diplomatic stalemates of the early 1910s. It moved rapidly, from the German advance through neutral Belgium and into France in August 1914, to the stalemate and miles of trenches on the Western Front. When the trench system was fully complete, it was virtually unbroken from near Nieuport on the English Channel across northern France and down to the Swiss border. An appalling technology of warfare, which led to an industrialized form of killing, rapidly dictated the progress of conflict (or lack of it) on both sides. Gas attacks were first used by the Germans against the Russians on the Eastern Front in early January 1915; they were launched against the French lines near Ypres in the west on 22 April. Particularly from the time of the Battle of the Somme in mid-1916, as the Anglo-Welsh poet David Jones acknowledged in his writing on this time, *In Parenthesis* (1937), 'things hardened into a more relentless, mechanical affair, took on a more sinister aspect'. Former ways of fighting, 'the intimate, continuing, domestic life of small contingents of men', were erased forever.

The belief on both sides of the conflict that the war would rapidly end soon gave way to reports of mass slaughter, as each army's attempts to break through either failed outright or led to only minor success at the cost of huge loss to life. Thousands and thousands who did not die suffered from shell-shock, which haunted them in their post-war lives, as it does Septimus Smith in Virginia Woolf's *Mrs Dalloway*. This shell-shock was caused by the high-explosive shells fired by field artillery which became readily available to all the armies involved by June 1915.[1] In the battles of the Marne (1914), the Somme and Verdun (1916), and Passchendaele (or the Third Battle of Ypres, 1917) there was a rapid progression in what Jones calls 'wholesale slaughter'. On the first day of the Somme alone, 1 July 1916, 19,000 British servicemen were killed, 38,000 injured. By September 1916, the first tanks were deployed in battle by a British High Command desperate for a break-through on the Somme.[2] Many texts at the time register and resist such traumatic and alienating developments, and question their purpose.

A botched civilization

The situation across these first two years of the war transformed itself swiftly from innocent conceptions of the nature of the conflict popularly shared across Europe at the outset, to the rapid growth in industry and technology which was necessary to sustain the war machines. National industries in Germany, Britain, and later America were swung into the production of armaments and ammunition for ever greater amounts of bombardment or ever more atrocious modes of killing, to force a breakthrough. After viewing the gunners firing on his first arrival at the Front ('out of their throats had sprung a dramatic flame'), the novelist and artist Wyndham Lewis meditates in his autobiographical *Blasting and Bombardiering* (1937) on the 'romance' of war. 'So we plunged immediately into the romance of battle. But all henceforth was romance. All this culminated of course in the scenery of the battlefields, like desolate lunar panoramas.'[3]

Lewis's typically cavalier argument that the war 'romance' continued, in spite of everything, throughout the four-year-long 'orchestration' of bombardment is, however, contradicted in other memoirs of the front line. These emphasize in fact the opposite – the utter insignificance of seeking to narrate the massively disturbing events of that time. The English poet Edmund Blunden, in the preliminary note to his prose memoir *Undertones of War* (1928), admits that 'I know that the experience to be sketched . . . is very local, limited, incoherent; that it is almost useless, in the sense that no one will read it who is not already aware of all the intimations and discoveries in it.'[4] The experience which he has to narrate is disordered and disorderly, dependent upon the vagaries of his memory as a soldier at the Front, more than on 'factual' record (p. 32). As with the view of cities shared by proto- and high-modernists discussed in the last chapter, these war memoirs emphasize the individual view, however chaotic, over the historical one. It is this that transforms the nature of such writing. Having seen the sentry next to him at Ypres in 1917 hit by a shell, Blunden records that (p. 182):

> in this vicinity a peculiar difficulty would exist for the artist to select the sights, faces, words, incidents, which characterized the time. The art is rather to collect them in their original form of incoherence.

The 'art', in other words, is in collecting together the body-parts, not in trying to reassemble them. Even at the ten years' distance between the ending of the war and the writing of his memoir, Blunden is unable to tell the difference between the small things that happened and the major ones. Details overwhelm his recollection, as they do the prose of his memoir. The ability of 'the artist' to select materials, and to order them into coherence, is lost in the shock of these events. Blunden's preliminary note is telling in its suggestion that this experience was shared not only by those fighting at the Front, but also by the potential readers of his work who had remained at home. The 'intimations and discoveries' made at the Front are known to all after the war, and yet he (and others) have no choice but 'to go over the ground again'. Blunden would refute the appropriateness of Lewis's idealizing term 'romance', but he would not deny that art was irrevocably altered ('local, limited, incoherent') by the conflict. The years running up to the war had seen the exhilaration of Marinetti's Futurist celebration of the machine, a celebration which acquired tragic irony in the light of the technology of killing on the battlefields. Those years had also seen the retrenchment in Anglo-American modernism of the Imagist 'movement'. What we will see in the early part of this chapter is how that world of artistic discovery was shattered by the events of August 1914, and how a recovery was attempted in the immediate post-war declarations of some of the major pre-war figures.

The style of Lewis's *Blasting and Bombardiering* is founded upon its early declaration that 'how like art is to war, I mean "modernist" art. They talk a lot about how a war just-finished effects art. But you will learn here how a war *about to start* can do the same thing' (p. 4). However, when later reflecting back upon the 'ferment of artistic intelligence' which had occurred in the west of Europe in the pre-war moments of 1914, Lewis is forced to conclude that the war had succeeded in bringing about the end of art itself: 'it altered the face of our civilization. It left the European nations impoverished, shell-shocked, discouraged and unsettled' (p. 258). Lewis is recalling that, between October 1918 and the spring of 1919, revolutions had broken out in Germany, Austria, and Hungary, following that which had taken place in Russia in 1917.⁵ The whole of the centre of Europe was suffering economic collapse and political crisis, something reflected in the nomination of 'Vienna London' as 'unreal' by T. S. Eliot in *The Waste Land* (1922, l. 376), and in the contrasting nostalgic evocation of the moment in the Hofgarten in section 1.

In such historical circumstances, the ambition of Eliot's key essays of the late 1910s and early 1920s, including 'Tradition and the Individual Talent' and 'The Metaphysical Poets', seem particularly concerned to address, as was Lewis, the question of what 'civilization' had suffered in the four years of World War One. Further, Eliot (like Pound) at this time sought to ask what 'civilization' in fact is, if it can lead to such devastation between nations. This is an issue Eliot had addressed in letters to his family back in America written towards the end of the war. It is also one that marked his growing national difference from them – a difference later confirmed in his naturalization as a British citizen in 1927. He wrote to his mother on 28 April 1918:

> Judging from American newspapers, the war seems to have affected the country not very seriously yet. I don't mean that it is not the chief subject of interest, but that it is *simply* the chief subject of interest, and not the obsessing nightmare that it is to Europe. And we can't make you realize three thousand miles away what all that means. Even with all your privations and difficulties. Your papers talk about the 'fight for civilization'; do they realize either what civilization means or the fight for it means? We are all immeasurably and irredeemably altered over here by the last three years.⁶

America had entered the war on the side of the Allies in mid-1917. Yet, for Eliot 'over here', the 'obsessing nightmare' of the war years seems very much like the purgatorial meanderings of the figures in *The Waste Land*. Eliot's quest to define 'what civilization means' is everywhere cut across by a sense of what it is that is destroyed in and through the conflict.

In the 1921 essay 'The Metaphysical Poets', Eliot famously establishes his ideal poetry as one in which ideas and physical sensations are united, where 'there is a direct sensuous apprehension of thought, or a recreation of thought into feeling'. He argues that this ideal inhered historically in English poetry 'of the seventeenth century (up to the Revolution)', after which a 'dissociation of sensibility' set in. He intended to mean the English Revolution of the seventeenth century, but the phrase re-echoes with the confirming strain of more recent revolutions, including the Russian. In the essay '*Ulysses*, Order, and Myth' (1923), Eliot praises James Joyce's (and Yeats's) use of the 'mythical method' of writing, which suggests 'a continuous parallel between contemporaneity and antiquity'. Yet he does so because such a method 'is simply a way of controlling, of ordering, of giving a shape and a significance to the immense panorama of futility and anarchy which is contemporary history'.[7] The shapelessness of history (Blunden's 'incoherence') can hope only to be partially restored through literary means which bridge such gaps or dissociations. This is the function of Eliot's conservative notion of 'tradition' in the 1919 'Tradition and the Individual Talent', whereby the true modern poem establishes continuities with a past which otherwise reveals breaches in 'civilization', such as that of the English Civil War or the recent war in Europe.

Similar tensions exist in the contemporary sequence of poems by Eliot's compatriot and mentor, Ezra Pound. This sequence formed Pound's 'farewell' to England, before his move to Paris in the early 1920s. 'Hugh Selwyn Mauberley (Life and Contacts)' appeared initially in 1920, and was revised by Pound several times. Mauberley is a persona who shares some aspects of Pound himself, but is in other ways very different from him. He therefore reflects something of the debates about personality and impersonality that resonate across this period. One of Pound's later revisions was to change the title of the original opening poem, 'Ode pour l'élection de son sépulcre' (meaning 'Ode for his choice of burial place') to 'E. P. Ode pour l'élection ...'. The change enabled Pound to pun on a classical poetic form (epode), but it also introduced Pound's own initials into the reader's mind, as though his presence stands behind Mauberley's own. The 'Ode' itself then represents a dismissal of Mauberley, who is now seen as a dead aesthete who, 'out of key with his time', had sought to resurrect 'the dead art', poetry. Yet, if this 'Ode' is a mini-requiem for Mauberley, it is clearly an ambivalent one. It does not necessarily agree with Mauberley's methods, but admires his attempts to 'resurrect' civilization in an age deaf to art.

Mauberley, in other words, emerges from the sequence as a whole as someone sharing some admirable Poundian/Imagist qualities of clarity and sculptural hardness of poetic form. But in other senses he is a version of an earlier Pound, one steeped in a late Romantic, pre-Raphaelite version of 'art for art's sake', focused on 'the obscure reveries / Of the inward gaze' rather than upon contemporary reality. Two poems in the sequence, 'Yeux glauques' and the following 'Siena mi fe; disfecemi Maremma', look back to the 1880s and 1890s, suggesting that Mauberley's aesthetics are tainted by a redundant passéism. What is shocking about Pound's sequence as a whole is the sudden interruption of such meditations about the technical features of modern art by several poems which bring sharply to the reader's attention the cost of human life on the battlefields in France: 'These fought in any case . . .'; 'There died a myriad'. The speaker's conclusion (and Pound's, presumably, in conceiving of the sequence as a farewell to the country he has lived in for twelve years), is that the cost was not worth it. The artistic debate in the sequence seems too self-involved in this historical light. The few 'broken statues' and 'battered books' which amount to 'civilization' have brought hideous new wastage and lies, 'hysterias, trench confessions', and little else.[8]

Pound's conclusion, unlike Eliot's essays reflecting upon the impact of the war, would seem to be that civilization from the perspective of England has achieved little – certainly not enough to warrant the sacrifice of 'the best', including some of his friends. More particularly, there would not seem to be available a version of a modern poetry which can resist contemporary demands in the modern capitalist marketplace and retain an aesthetic integrity. Mauberley's aestheticism is outmoded, but nothing replaces it other than the uncertain note of mockery and lament that comes through in these poems. Pound's sequence ends in the world of Eliot's early poetry, a literary salon and vague dalliance which is 'out of key' with the modern world of newspapers and of 'the sale of half-hose' stockings. As my next chapter will discuss further, Pound's attempts to resolve these dichotomies between past and present, 'civilization' and economics, would consist of the fifty-year quest embodied in his epic sequence *The Cantos*, upon which he was already working by this time.

But the tensions around aestheticism in 'Hugh Selwyn Mauberley', as with other tensions in his writing, had already been founded in Pound's pre-war notions of modernity, in Imagism (discussed in Chapter 1), and in his subsequent involvements. These are tensions about the relation of a classical art to expressive consciousness which were prevalent at the time, as we shall now see. For it was Lewis's assertion in *Blasting and Bombardiering* that it is not only in the aftermath of war that art changes; it changes also in those moments when a war is '*about to start*'. The first number of Lewis's so-called Vorticist magazine *Blast* had appeared in June 1914, drawing together an eclectic range of writers from Pound to Rebecca West and Ford Madox Ford (there was only one more issue, in

July 1915, which carried the first printing of poems by Eliot in England). The magazine carried much of Lewis's own writing and was notable for its inclusion of visual art, by Lewis, Edward Wadsworth, Jacob Epstein, and the sculpture of the Frenchman Henri Gaudier-Brzeska amongst others. The titles of some of Lewis's art included give the tenor of its approach to the contemporary *status quo*. The acerbity of 'Plan of War' and 'Slow Attack' is consonant with the magazine's ambition to assert the vital individualism of the artist against contemporary constraints of class and the bourgeoisie. To this end, the printed 'Manifesto' includes proclamation 4: 'We fight first on one side, then on the other, but always for the SAME cause, which is neither side or both sides or ours.'[9]

The magazine's confrontational use of slogans and various typefaces advertises its difference from other arts journals of the time, and its concern to defeat the expectations of the usual readership. As with Imagism, Ezra Pound proved the primary propagandist and historian of the new movement of Vorticism. Once the war had started and Gaudier-Brzeska had been killed in 1915, Pound also pre-emptively reflected upon the place of Vorticism itself in modern literary history. He was anxious in his recollection of the movement to establish continuities between Vorticism and Imagism, yet also to establish key differences. Vorticism both is and is not Imagism in a new guise, in other words. Pound emphasizes rather the dynamism that carries Vorticism away from Imagism's associations with Symbolism (which I also discussed above in Chapter 1).

He declared in an essay of September 1914, reprinted in full in his memoir *Gaudier-Brzeska*, that:

> the 'image' [has] . . . something to do with mood. The image is not an idea. It is a radiant node or cluster; it is what I can, and must perforce, call a VORTEX, from which, and through which, and into which, ideas are constantly rushing.[10]

Vorticism represents, in other words, the image put into motion and constantly caught up in a swirl of 'ideas' and 'moods'. This subtle distinction between *literary* movements perhaps masks too much the real exhilaration brought for Pound by the alliance with Lewis around *Blast*. For him, 'the image' as conceived by the movement of 1912, as the means by which modern poetry might be returned to a paradoxically new essentialism, is now located alongside parallel developments in the visual arts and in sculpture. The shattered belief in the Mauberley sequence that, after the war, civilization amounted to little more than a few 'broken statues' is, from this perspective, the more poignant.

The war poets

For British poets who served at the front line during the First World War, the experiences they underwent wrought a huge change in the form and content of their poetry. The relation of such changes to the high experimentation of Anglo-American and Irish modernism is not immediate. Many of these poets evolved their modern style in response to the horrors at the Front where they often died. But the war poets are central to the enduring mythology of World War One, a mythology deeply embedded in that of the modernist movement itself. It is for this reason that the war poets appear here. The kinds of writing they were engaged upon before enlisting, writing often in a pastoral vein, is frequently brought up against the brutal and alienating realities of newly technologized modern warfare in ways that parallel the clash between tradition and modernity elsewhere in this period. These writers worked initially in a Romantic or post-Romantic style, influenced by English poets such as Blake, Keats, and (the still-living) Hardy. But they found the smooth rhythms of their verse interrupted by what Wilfred Owen, in one of the most famous poems about the Front, called 'The shrill, demented choirs of wailing shells'.[11]

Owen's echoing here of a line from Keats's ode 'To Autumn' ('Then in a wailful choir the small gnats mourn') is illustrative of the interruption which the war represented for these poets steeped in the native tradition. Keats's celebration of the round of the seasons, with its lament for transience, has been overwhelmed by the excruciating and maddening life in the trenches on the Somme. Historians of the war, like John Keegan, have noted the resemblance between the nature of the pastoral landscape in France in which the fighting was taking place, and that of certain milder landscapes in the south of England. The scene at the Front was, therefore, a relatively familiar one to the soldiers in the early stages of the war (later it was to turn through the shelling into that 'lunar landscape' mentioned by Lewis). This familiarity was particularly remarkable for those poets writing out of, and in full knowledge of, the strengths of the English poetic tradition. Poems like Siegfried Sassoon's 'The Last Meeting' draw a distinct parallel between the scene in France and a recognizable pastoral note from the English tradition.[12] Seeking to commune with the spirit of a dead friend, the speaker in Sassoon's poem seeks in memory the woods where they walked, where 'I found a holy dimness, and the peace of sanctuary'. The speaker strikes a note reminiscent of Wordsworth's sense of the holiness of nature in works like 'Nutting'. And yet that familiarity only serves to exacerbate the sense of shock which greets the destruction of the now French countryside by heavy artillery, a shock which everywhere in this poetry leads to a nostalgia for what Owen, in 'Anthem for Doomed Youth', calls 'the sad shires' of England itself.

As for Owen, so for Sassoon, these memories form a counterweight to the horrors of the current scene – one that often comments ironically upon it. In Sassoon's 'Break of Day', a soldier in a 'dank, musty dug-out' who is about to take part in an attack in which there is a high likelihood that he will be killed, dreams of 'a dusty Sussex lane / In quiet September'. This is a lane in which 'All things that he has loved are in his sight / The places where his happiness has been / Are in his eyes, his heart, and they are good' (p. 91). More directly than with Owen, we have here a distinct sense of the literal dislocation enforced upon the individual by the war, the destruction of all remnants of benevolent experience. Sassoon's ideal peaceful state is therefore figured as a return to an Edenic place, which bears the marks of the cultivated landscape of England. In 'To Victory', the poet calls for a return of colour to counteract the greys and browns of the barren landscapes of the battlefield: 'Return to greet me, colours that were my joy, / Not in the woeful crimson of men slain, / But shining as a garden'. The speaker yearns for 'Radiance through living roses, spires of green / Rising in young-limbed copse' (p. 9). This ideal elsewhere is, more often than not, confirmed in its remoteness and inaccessibility by the action the soldiers are involved in.[13] In 'The Distant Song', the opening scene and emotion are familiar, as 'He stood in the gray trench and longed for home', but, on hearing a blackbird singing behind the German lines, he is 'suddenly' aware that it is spring, 'So he stood staring from his ghastly trench, / While Paradise was in the distant song' (p. 53).

Much of the power of these poems of the First World War comes from the dramatization of such contrasts. These are contrasts between England and the Front, between the assumed radiant past and the horrific present, between pastoral and the 'angry guns', between hitherto-held beliefs and the gasped-out questionings of faith of the dying. Sassoon more than most dramatizes the scepticism about Christian faith which arose amid the slaughter. In 'Christ and the Soldier', for instance, a soldier straggling behind the marching column is imagined to have an exchange of conversation with a wayside crucifix. Christ is seen as showing his own wounds to the soldier and reassuring him: 'I made you for the mysteries. / Beyond all battles moves the Paraclete.' But Sassoon's common man is unswayed by such unseen beneficence. 'Forsaken Jesus dreamed in desolate day', and the crucifix is used as an observation post by the troops. Finally, Christ is silenced. As the soldier makes to leave, '"O God," he groaned, "why ever was I born?" ... / The battle boomed, and no reply came back' (pp. 34–5). The divine purpose of this conflict, if such there is, is not revealed to those embroiled in it, and this heightens the desolation of the scene.

Sassoon's 'Christ and the Soldier' might be set in insightful contrast to Rupert Brooke's sonnet 'The Soldier', from his sequence '1914'. There, Brooke's blithe assurance 'That there's some corner of a foreign field / That is forever England' suggests that there is a reciprocity between 'the thoughts by England given' and 'the eternal mind'. This reciprocity will resolve itself for the dead soldier as 'gentleness, / In hearts at peace, under an English heaven.'[14] Brooke's sequence from the opening year of the war (he never lived to see action, dying on the way to the conflict) suggests a continuing courtliness that predates the vicious trench warfare which had set in by the end of 1914. Brooke's final 'gentleness' is also a traditional gentlemanliness, one in which a knight-like respect is paid to the individual soldier, however low in rank. This is a soldier who in the poem noticeably receives a decent burial, in contrast with the later scenes of unburied corpses littering no-man's land between the trenches.

Sassoon's experience of trench warfare suggests an opposite view. In the mockingly titled 'The Poet as Hero' we are told that 'you've asked me why / Of my old, sweet silliness I've repented'. We gather that this was once a poet of precisely that mythologized courtliness typical of Brooke's soldier, as in 'once I sought the Grail, / Riding in armour bright, serene and strong'. But now all is utterly changed, 'For lust and senseless hatred make me glad, / and my killed friends are with me where I go' (p. 50). The 'absolution' which this exemplary 'poet' offers the reader is a sheer disillusioning of the audience about the realities of modern warfare, where nothing any longer is sacred. Running through Sassoon's work, as in the poem ironically called 'Base Details', is a hatred for the feudal hierarchies of army life. This is a feudalism in which the common soldiers are sacrificed through blunders made by the officer class, a class whose rhetoric ('we've lost heavily in this last scrap') is punctured by the realities Sassoon gives elsewhere in stark detail.

A similar attack upon the emptiness of a former faith in honour and patriotism is the subject of one of Owen's most famous works, 'Dulce et Decorum Est'. The dreadful contrast between the resonant Latin of the title (meaning 'it is sweet and right to die for one's country') and the poem's opening lines is grotesque: 'Bent double, like old beggars under sacks, / Knock-kneed, coughing like hags, we cursed through sludge'. Owen's description of a gas attack here reveals an unimaginable enormity of hellishness (one victim has a 'hanging face, like a devil's sick of sin'). By the end of the poem, the Latin tag of the title is dismissed as 'the old Lie', as something unreasoning in the current context of warfare.

However, whilst the content of such Owen poems strains against the traditional formal qualities of the verse, those qualities do not wholly give way before experience. The traditional decorousness of poetry, its mannerliness, is rather adjusted and challenged by the extreme experiences registered there. 'Dulce et Decorum Est' is formed by two sonnets placed together. There is, however, a brokenness about the double-sonnet form of 'Dulce et Decorum Est' which might be taken as *performative*. Owen, in his most extreme rebuttal of the emptiness of the various blind rhetorical gestures that were at this time being used to justify the random deaths of hundreds of thousands of troops, shows traditional form operating under unique strain.[15] The first sonnet is fairly recognizable as such, with its traditional eight/six line split between the two parts of the description. But the next two lines, the 'start' of the second sonnet, have become detached, and the horror of the nightmare vision of the gassed soldier seen by the narrator is isolated in its fullness (p. 117):

> In all my dreams, before my helpless sight,
> He plunges at me, guttering, choking, drowning.

Owen confirms for the addressee of the poem (the writer of children's popular and patriotic verses, Jesse Pope), who is being chided within it, that it is the dreadful nightmares which such sights invoke that prove the barbaric vanity of such phrases as 'dulce et decorum est'.

As in this poem, traditional form is both there to be discovered and is not, being under threat from the appalling content of the writing. Similar points might be made about Owen's famous formal 'invention' in the poems he wrote about experience at the Front, that of *pararhyme*, a kind of half-rhyme, where the lines both do and do not display a harmony between each other. Several of Owen's most famous works deploy similar-sounding words at the end of lines which are not, however, full rhymes. In 'Strange Meeting', for instance, we find rhymes like escaped/scooped, or eyes/bless, or laughed/left. Once again, there is a ghostly retention of a recognizable strong and complete form to the poetry, which is also, in these extreme situations, under threat of being broken apart. Here the recognition that the faceless and nameless enemy is in fact a human being as well, runs directly contrary to propaganda at the time (p. 125). The body of the poem is no longer as immediately whole as the English tradition up to this point might lead one to expect it to be. The Romantic inheritance from Keats to Yeats, which Owen was imbued with, starts to fall apart in these conditions (although it continued as a tendency in his writing to nearly the end, in poems being drafted in the last year of his life like 'To Eros' and 'I am the Ghost of Shadwell Stair').

It is not too large a leap from the formal context of such poems to consider Sassoon and Owen's treatment of those men maimed at the Front. The sense of the distance of the Front from the known world, although a distance enforced by a familiarity in the pastoralism of its scene, becomes in poems considering wounded soldiers a sense of the distance from their peers that the maiming has enforced upon their future lives. Sassoon's deeply ambiguous and ironic 'The One-Legged Man' relishes describing the man's return to familiar scenes at home, but turns darker in its final lines (p. 37), where

> He hobbled blithely through the garden gate,
> And thought: 'Thank God they had to amputate!'

Owen's greater compassion comes through in his poem for victims of shell-shock, 'Mental Cases' ('Who are these? Why sit they here in twilight?'), and in his poem for a wheelchair-bound veteran, 'Disabled', which sees the man kept literally remote from former scenes at home: 'Now, he will spend a few sick years in institutes'. The legless man's lack of bitterness for those who maimed him is part of the extraordinary sympathy displayed here ('Germans he scarcely thought of; all their guilt, / And Austria's, did not move him'). But this only adds to the sadness at his neglect, as 'Tonight he noticed how the women's eyes / Passed from him to the strong men that were whole' (pp. 146, 152).

The Home Front

Owen's sensitivity towards those maimed at the Front, and their world of horrors which cannot be translated back into life at home in England, forms part of the context of two works of fiction reflecting on the experience of the war. Rebecca West's *The Return of the Soldier* (1918) and D. H. Lawrence's *Lady Chatterley's Lover* (1928) both review the impact of trench experience upon those left behind at home, principally upon gender relations. Both novels display similar contrasts to those already discussed with regard to the poetry that was being written immediately from the experiences of the Front by British soldier-poets. There is a sense of remoteness but familiarity in their returned soldiers' experience. West's shell-shocked soldier suffers from a loss of memory which means that he thinks he remains in love with his first love, Margaret, rather than with his wife, Kitty. His character and situation, though, are very much associated by West with the house and garden in Harrow-weald in which he has lived for a long time. His cousin Jenny, herself more than a little in love with him, reflects early on in the book about the improvements which have been made to the house in his absence:

I was sure that we were preserved from the reproach of luxury because
we had made a fine place for Chris, one little part of the world that
was, so far as surfaces could make it so, good enough for his amazing
goodness.[16]

Chris is portrayed as standing in his home doorway 'delighting in just whatever way the weather looked in the familiar frame of things, how our rooms
burned with many coloured brightness' (pp. 16–17).

As the inevitable tensions grow between Kitty and Margaret, Jenny again
has recourse to the sense that, looking at the house, 'If everything else goes
there is always this to fall back on' (p. 120). Yet, in the novel's harrowing
final pages, when Margaret has accepted the inevitable parting of the ways,
and the impossibility of recouping the missed love she and Chris shared,
such assurance itself gives way before the dreadfulness of Chris's state. In
the failure of this love, Margaret and Jenny discover an intimacy ('We
kissed, not as women, but as lovers do') which predicts the post-war
nostalgia for a romance with Sally Seton from Woolf's *Mrs Dalloway*.
(West's returned soldier looks forward to Septimus Smith in Woolf's novel,
the shell-shock victim whose marriage is destroyed by the conflict and who
eventually commits suicide.) Walking back across the lawn, Chris looks at
the 'overarching' house as though he hates it, and he wears a 'dreadful
decent smile' (p. 187):

When we had lifted the yoke of our embraces from his shoulders he
would go back to that flooded trench in Flanders under that sky more
full of flying death than clouds.

The home place is tainted by the experiences from the Front through the
maiming of one who was most related to it. Yet, at the same time, he cannot
return to a communion with that idyllic place of his first romance either.

An additional strain in *The Return of the Soldier*, one further destabiliz-
ing relations, is that provided by class. The years running up to the war had
provided an all-embracing stratification of English society for the first time
in history, so that many cultural and social pursuits began to be labelled
along class lines. Chris's shell-shocked return to his first love, and ignorance
of his marriage to the middle-class Kitty, is the more shocking in that it is a
return also to a cross-class relationship his marriage had eradicated. Similar
cross-class tensions of course run through Lawrence's *Lady Chatterley's
Lover*, whose tale is very much that signalled in the scenario of Owen's
poem 'Disabled'. Here, the central female character, Connie, does overlook
her wounded and incapacitated ex-soldier husband for the 'whole' man,
Mellors, the gamekeeper on Sir Clifford Chatterley's estate.

The relationship with the gamekeeper, with its explicit use of Anglo-Saxon words for sexual organs, marks also a return to a more ancient version of the nation itself. Lawrence had suffered under the Defence of the Realm Act during the war. The Act, which had first been passed on 8 August 1914, was initially aimed to prevent the passing on of information that would aid the German cause. Across the war it was continually modified until it covered regulations governing food control, air-raid precautions, and, most importantly, censorship of the press and of books likely to damage national morale. In this atmosphere, Lawrence's novel *The Rainbow* had been put on trial for obscenity and the publishers, Methuen, ordered to burn all copies on 13 November 1915. It is as though in his last novel, *Lady Chatterley's Lover*, which returns to the aftermath of those years, Lawrence was eager to dare the charge again, but to validate his actions through a claim to the historical authenticity and essential Englishness of such descriptions and attitudes to sexuality.

Mellors's cottage in the wood is situated in 'a remnant from the great forest where Robin Hood hunted' and has 'some of the mystery of wild old England'.[17] Yet this 'remnant' has been further 'denuded' during the war, as its trees have been cut down to supply timber for the trenches in France (p. 42). The novel displays the way in which England, and the relationship of the English to the land, have been disturbed by the war. Sir Clifford can supply no heir to the family estate, and the seemingly natural continuities that had held for the nation across history have been forever disturbed. The author interrupts his own text at one point, as Connie travels into Uthwaite (p. 156):

> England, my England! But which is *my* England? The stately homes of England make good photographs, and create an illusion of a connection with the Elizabethans ... Now they are being pulled down ... This is history. One England blots out another ... the industrial England blots out the agricultural England. One meaning blots out another ... and the continuity is not organic, but mechanical.

But the dejection at the 'blotting out' of past national selves is exacerbated by what Connie reflects upon at another point as 'the bruise of war ... the bruise of the false and inhuman war' (p. 50). 'Mechanical' here alludes not just to Lawrence's objection to the effect upon lives of industrialism, but also to the machine-fed brutalities of the war. From the 1880s onwards, rural landed society had been under threat from the new international finance filtered through the City of London, and had 'by the 1900s been largely pincered out by democracy and agricultural depression, and was being replaced by "delocalised irresponsible wealth"'.[18] In Lawrence's

Midland mining country, as viewed in this late novel, those ancient links
have been further loosened by the conflict of 1914–18. It is these links, and
the issue of national inheritance ('which is *my* England?') that had preoccupied Lawrence during the war itself, and affected deeply his move towards
a more radical conception of character and of the form of the novel in the
years succeeding the war.

Lawrence's semi-autobiographical novel *Kangaroo* (1923) both exemplifies the narrative disruptions brought about by this history ('Bits', one
chapter is called) and reflects upon what the war changed. In narrating the
nightmare undergone by the Lawrence-like central character, Somers, as he
is called up for medical tests before service and as he is hounded by the
authorities, Lawrence interjects essay-like passages into the text summing
up the view that 'It was in 1915 the old world ended':

> In the winter of 1915–16 the spirit of the old London collapsed, the city,
> in some way, perished, perished from being a heart of the world, and
> became a vortex of broken passions, lusts, hopes, fears, and horrors.
> The integrity of London collapsed, and the genuine debasement began,
> the unspeakable baseness of the press and the public voice.[19]

For Lawrence, the failure of the Liberal government under Asquith, and its
replacement by the extremely nationalistic '*John Bull* government of '16,
'17, '18', the war-coalition led by Lloyd George, inflicted a conformity upon
the national character from which it had never recovered: 'It was at home
the world was lost' (p. 217). The immediate cause of this disruption, as he
sees it, was the Zeppelin raids on the country. Bombs had been dropped by
these airships in small raids throughout the spring of 1915, but by the beginning of June they were becoming serious enough for citizens in London and
the south-east to become worried. On the 18th the police issued for the first
time instructions as to how to behave in a raid.[20]

Lawrence, whose difficult personal and financial circumstances at the
time meant that he was constantly on the move from loaned country
cottages to London and back, witnessed one such raid. He reported it to one
of his patrons, Lady Ottoline Morrell, in a letter of 9 September:

> I cannot get over it, that the moon is not the queen of the sky by night,
> and the stars the lesser lights. It seems the Zeppelin is in the zenith of
> the night, golden like the moon, having taken control of the sky; and
> the bursting shells are the lesser lights.
>
> So it seems our cosmos has burst, burst at last.[21]

In the months preceding the war, Lawrence was revising a long manuscript
then called *The Wedding Ring* into what would soon become two novels,

The Rainbow (1915) and *Women in Love* (1920). In the process, he had famously recognized when writing to a friend that the nature of characterization in fiction must change: 'You musn't look in my novel for the old stable *ego* – of the character. There is another *ego*, according to which the individual is unrecognisable' (p. 282). The recognition marked the beginning of Lawrence's exploration of the non-public, non-social self, in contradistinction from earlier novelists' practice, and his brooding upon the hidden nature of selfhood. With the violation of the integrity of the country through the air-raids, and the consequent 'baseness' of the 'authorized' political public voice for him, this sense of the unsettlement of the 'old stabilities' took on a further, national, dimension.

Writing during a stay at Morrell's country house at Garsington near Oxford in the autumn of 1915, Lawrence reflected in another letter (p. 378):

> I am so sad, for my country, for this great wave of civilization . . . this house . . . is England – my God, it breaks my soul – their England . . . the past, the great past, crumbling down.

That sense of the 'pathos of old things passing away and no new things coming' overshadowed the novel Lawrence worked on during a beleaguered retreat with his German wife, Frieda, to Cornwall in 1917. *Women in Love* does not directly address the war, but it carries much of that unsettledness which Lawrence registered in his letters at the time. In the contrasted relationships between two couples, Gerald Crich and Gudrun Brangwen, Rupert Birkin and Ursula Brangwen, there is much of that contrast between 'old things' and 'new things' Lawrence drew in the 1915 letter. In the Rupert and Ursula relationship, even, we discover that quest for an articulation of the 'new' which Lawrence felt keenly that public discourses at this time particularly refused to offer.

The dramatic form in which the novel is cast means that the 'new' definitions the central characters seek to achieve about the possibilities for a new relation between them emerge from debate and conflict. In seeking to describe his feelings for Ursula, Birkin utters some Lawrencean commonplaces, such as that 'There is a real impersonal me, that is beyond love, beyond any emotional relationship.'[22] But, under Ursula's hurt mockery at this resistance to true understanding between them ('Sophistries!'), Birkin is forced to concede the aspirational nature of his ideal (p. 217):

> 'Say you love me, say "my love" to me,' she pleaded . . .
> 'I love you right enough,' he said, grimly. 'But I want it to be something else.'
> 'But why? But why?' she insisted.[23]

The novel's celebration of the new possibilities of their relationship is symbolized by their leaving their jobs in England and escaping to the warmth of Italy. But this is, however, held in unresolved tension with the equal and opposite possibility contained in the lonely icy death of Gerald in the Alps after the failure of his relationship with Gudrun. 'The industrial magnate' Gerald, who has insisted obstinately that he be educated in Germany rather than his native country (p. 294), is imbued with the German philosopher Friedrich Nietzsche's central notion of the Will to Power.[24]

The Will to Power was Nietzsche's explanation of what it is that motivates us, given the lack of our freedom to dictate and choose our actions. In *Women in Love*, written at a time of Lawrence's greatest depression about the historical manifestations of that Will not just from Germany but within his own country, Gerald assumes a similarly ambivalent fascination. As seen by his soon-to-be-lover Gudrun, 'he was really impersonal, he had the fineness of an elegant piece of machinery. He was too cold, too destructive to care really for women, too great an egotist' (p. 176). But Birkin continues to insist to the end of the book that he could have established a friendship with Gerald which would counterbalance his love for Ursula, and in this lies the novel's final tragic note. After Gerald's ironic death in the mountains so essential to Nietzsche's imagined power-driven supermen, Birkin continues to assert his belief, in despite of Ursula's continuing mockery (p. 583).

At a time of international conflict, therefore, Lawrence typically uses his explorations of human relations to explore tensions being worked out elsewhere. His sense of irresolution, embodied in the dramatic form the novel adopts (the final chapter is called 'Exeunt', the final stage direction of classic drama), perhaps reflects the recognition that at such a time the positions adopted in the debate by the main characters are simply speechifying. For all the *talk* about 'new' relations, the novel cannot articulate them; Lawrence's unsettledness about the state of the nation, of character, and of relations between the sexes, in this time of war cannot articulate more than an unspecific hope against the ruptured drift of history.

There is a similar recognition in Ford Madox Ford's novel *The Last Post* (1928). This novel completes Ford's sequence of works tracing the fortunes of a country house and family at the time of World War One, called *Parade's End*. In earlier (pre-war) parts of the sequence, the broodings of the central figure, Christopher Tietjens, include a wittily parodic take on the relationship with the English landscape. Tietjens meditates on dialect words ('racy of the soil') and traditions which were also Lawrence's nostalgic preoccupation in his last novel: 'Walk, then, through the field, gallant youth and fair maid, minds cluttered up with all these useless anodynes for thought, quotation, imbecile epithets!'[25] Tietjens' own relationship to the country, though, has been disturbed by his disinheritance from the family house, Groby, due to his split from his wife. The resulting disturbance remains with him through the war, during which he seeks a retrospective relationship to an idealized version of the country, just as the so-called war poets, including Owen, Sassoon, and Gurney, had done. At Tietjens' post on the front line in *A Man Could Stand Up–* (1926, p. 613),

> The name *Bemerton* suddenly came on his tongue. Yes, Bemerton, Bemerton, Bemerton was George Herbert's parsonage. Bemerton, outside Salisbury ... The cradle of the race as far as our race was worth thinking about. He imagined himself standing up on a little hill, a lean contemplative parson ...

By the final book in the series, *The Last Post*, set after the Armistice in November 1918, however, Tietjens' understanding of irresolvable personal conflict and failure has been mapped onto the nation at large, and the fate of the family's country house becomes symbolic of a larger distress.

The phrase 'times have changed' tolls across this novel. Tietjens had worked for the Finance Ministry before the war, and his vision of the post-war world is sensitive to the economic shifts away from former practices. In the wake of America's entry into the war in 1917, he realizes that post-war America will move in on the 'ruined' (financially and psychologically) England. 'He predicted the swarms of Americans buying up old things. Offering fabulous prices. He was right. The trouble was they did not pay when they offered the fabulous prices' (pp. 883–4). Christopher's chances of survival in this world, as a second-hand furniture dealer, are, therefore, precarious. His new partner, the militant suffragette Valerie Wannop (times have changed former antagonisms between opposing political stances for the Tory Tietjens as well), is expecting their first child.

Yet, more pertinently for the fate of England in this changed historical situation, as Tietjens predicted, the country house Groby has had to be let out to Americans, since the family finances have suffered so much across the war years. Groby Great Tree, a symbol of family continuities on the land like the wych-elm at E. M. Forster's *Howards End*, is cut down by the new tenants. In the process of dragging it away, part of the house is destroyed, including Christopher's childhood nursery. Like Lawrence, therefore, Ford sees the effect of the war directly upon England itself; the victor in the international conflict will take generations to recover from the trauma inflicted by it.

Like Lawrence and other modernists preoccupied by the significance of individual and private lives in the alien public space, Ford figures the trauma of the historical conflict very much in terms of a trauma in personal relationships. Tietjens finds himself transferred from a reserve camp to the Front, because of a hotel brawl he has had with one of his wife's former lovers. In a conversation with a family friend Major-General Campion before his departure he rejects the notion that his difficulty might lead him to commit suicide, as his father had done (p. 529):

> 'No, sir. I shan't do that … you see how bad for one's descendants suicide is … Military operations sweep on. But my problem will remain the same whether I'm here or not. For it's insoluble. It's the problem of the relations of the sexes.'

A similar concatenation between history and personal circumstances takes place in Ford's earlier novel, *The Good Soldier* (1915). The marriage of the novel's American narrator, John Dowell, has remained unconsummated, his wife proclaiming herself to suffer from a dangerous heart condition. But, as the novel progresses, it is revealed that she has had in fact a series of lovers, most notably 'the good soldier' of the book's title, Edward Ashburnham. Ashburnham and his wife had first met the Dowells on a trip to a German spa town on 4 August 1904, and the novel is based around this setting upon its protagonists' annual return. The fourth of August is also Dowell's wife Florence's birthday, and the date upon which she lost her virginity. It will also be the date of her suicide, depressed at the loss of Edward to his illicit passion for a young woman in his and his wife's care. The fourth of August 1914 was also the date upon which Germany invaded Belgium, and there has of course been much conflicting speculation about Ford's use of this apocalyptic date as the one upon which the novel's central trauma rests.

However that may be, it is symptomatic of the way in which the novels under discussion present meditations upon specifically English traditions and characteristics. Such characteristics are present, for example, in Ashburnham's enigmatic conventionality – 'Edward was the normal man … conventions and traditions work blindly' – as under threat through personal trauma at this particular historical moment.[26] What is telling about the plot of *The Good Soldier*, completed in the early stage of the war, is the sense that the war had a particular unsettling effect upon relations between the sexes. This is true also of later works reflecting upon its impact including *Lady Chatterley's Lover* and Ezra Pound's 1919 poetic sequence 'Homage to Sextus Propertius'. The tragedy of World War One is reflected by the 'sex war' being enacted at home. In male novelists' eyes, the sense of tension between the sexes is clearly exacerbated by the new-found freedom and independence amongst women brought about amongst other things by the rise of the women's movement (discussed in Chapter 5) in the immediate pre-war years.

In *Death of a Hero*, the 1929 novel partly about a soldier at the Front by
the former Imagist poet Richard Aldington, the hero in question is torn
between his relationship with one woman, Elizabeth, and with another, her
best friend Fanny. In recounting George Winterbourne's feelings at Officer's
Training Camp in 1917, Aldington dramatizes typical tensions at the time:

> He was living a sort of double nightmare – the nightmare of the War
> and the nightmare of his own life. Each seemed inextricably inter-
> woven. His personal life became intolerable because of the War, and the
> War became intolerable because of his own life. The strain imposed on
> him – or which he imposed upon himself – must have been terrific.[27]

The three-part novel enables Aldington to include sections on George's life
from 1890 onwards, as well as on his relations with the two women before
the war. These are sections which operate uneasily at the level of a social
comedy, jarring against the brutal realities of the Front narrated in the final
section. Amidst these caustic ironies, however, is a misogynistic sense that
behind the 'sex war' of the novel is the women's schooling in modern ideas
(p. 24):

> Elizabeth and Fanny . . . adjusted to the war with marvellous precision
> and speed, just as they afterwards adjusted themselves to the post-war.
> They both had that rather hard efficiency of the war and post-war
> female, veiling the ancient predatory and possessive instincts of sex
> under a skilful smoke-barrage of Freudian and Havelock Ellis
> theories. To hear them talk theoretically was most impressive. They
> were terribly at ease upon the Zion of sex, abounding in inhibitions,
> dream symbolism, complexes, sadism, repressions, masochism,
> Lesbianism, sodomy, etcetera.

The irony of this suggested division within the women themselves, between
a verbal openness and sophistication about personal life, and the repression
of their own 'predatory and possessive instincts', is what the novel reveals.
The emotional side of love and sex, the 'slip-slop messes' which their sophistication and reading in sex theory (Ellis) and psychoanalysis is aimed at
avoiding, is of course what entangles them. The war, in the end, offers a way
out of the irresolvable situation. It allows Elizabeth and Fanny, who have
themselves become estranged across the book, to agree on one thing:
'George had degenerated terribly since joining the army, and there was no
knowing to what preposterous depths of Tommydom he might fall' (p. 228).
The final section of the text, which, barring a dismal period of leave in
which George recognizes his failed relations with both women, is set at the
Front, offers a separate space in which this ironically nominated 'hero' can

at last come into his own. But it is soon brought to an end with his death near the Belgian border in the last days of the war, in an action to mop up retreating German soldiers. Aldington's recollections through the book seem wearily unable, therefore, to bring its various forces together; the two 'nightmares' of the personal life and the war remain interwoven, and the only release is through the 'hero's' unheroic death.

Death of a Hero, like the other novels mentioned in this section of the chapter, represents a familiar tension at the time: a new sense of uncertainty about relations between the sexes. The historian Arthur Marwick has described the hedonistic atmosphere which marked the war years, where returning troops were treated to a newly liberated blend of night-clubs, bawdy theatre, and comparatively open sexual relations. This atmosphere took its own toll, inevitably, though, upon sustained relationships:

> The safest generalization about the First World War would be that it was a time of powerfully heightened emotional activity and responses. Often this just meant earlier and hastier marriages ... there was a threefold increase in the number of divorces 'made absolute' ... This did represent a fundamental cracking in the cement of conventional society as the Victorians understood it.[28]

Part of the modernism of the texts at the time is the way in which they represent that 'fundamental cracking'. Most significantly, perhaps, the war brought a real change in women's status as they took over vital jobs vacated by men who went to the Front, particularly after the introduction of conscription, whereby men were forced to enlist for service, in 1916. Women were already increasingly taking up employment before the war, but the years 1914–18 saw over a million women working in engineering, munitions, transport, and commerce, and on the land, for the first time. There was a shift from domestic service to other employment which was never to be reversed, and women suddenly found themselves independent in new ways. The average wage for working women nearly doubled from pre-war levels.[29]

One of the early literary works to register this shift into uncertainty is D. H. Lawrence's symbolic story 'The Fox', an extended version of an earlier work of the same name, which was completed in 1921. Two women, March and Banford, who have worked on a farm during the war, have their relationship and lives disrupted in the immediate post-war period by the arrival of Henry, a soldier returned from the Front. A fox has been stealing chickens from the women's hen-coop, and Henry tries to kill it for them. But, for March, who has created an odd alliance with the fox, Henry is also fox-like, disturbing her unconscious and threatening her. 'The Fox' is, therefore, a working-out of these equivalences, as Henry seeks to steal March away with him, achieving it at the end of the story with his seemingly accidental killing of Banford.

What is striking about 'The Fox', in connection with the disturbance of established relations I have been describing here, is the note of irresolution upon which the tale ends. Henry wishes to possess March, to take her away to Canada and a new life, but she resists his final attempts at reassurance:

'You'll feel better when once we get overseas . . .'
'Shall I?' she said . . . 'Yes. I may. I can't tell . . .'
'If only we could go soon!' he said, with pain in his voice.[30]

Lawrence seems to recognize here that those issues which had dominated in *The Rainbow* and *Women in Love*, issues about the nature and possibilities of relationships between the sexes in the modern world, remain more unresolved at the end of the war than before. The male's possessiveness seems redundant and irrelevant to these changed conditions, in which women's lives, aspirations, and experiences have become different. As a result, the tale ends uncertainly and inconclusively, with little sense of the likely achievement of union in the future.

Ireland

In the years before the First World War, the greatest threats to the status quo in Britain had come, on the one hand, from the rise of the women's movement (discussed in Chapter 5 below) and, on the other, from the issue of Home Rule for Ireland. A succession of attempts to establish a basis for Irish independence had been made from the time of Prime Minister Gladstone in the 1880s. Gladstone had been persuaded to adopt the cause of Irish independence by the Irish nationalist leader at Westminster, Charles Stewart Parnell. But in 1891 Parnell was dead, disgraced by his adulterous relationship with a married woman and hounded by the Catholic Church in Ireland. Therefore, by the time of Asquith's Liberal government in the early 1910s, the situation remained unresolved. Three sessions of parliament were unsuccessfully devoted to the matter in 1911, with the motions each time being blocked in the House of Lords. In 1912 a third Home Rule Bill was introduced, with a two-year timetable allowed for its passage through the legislature. In the meantime, Ulster Unionists in the north of the island of Ireland, who resisted the notion of Irish independence from Britain, took matters into their own hands and formed a paramilitary force, the Ulster Volunteers, which numbered 100,000. The Protestants signed up in huge numbers to the so-called Ulster Covenant drawn up by Sir Edward Carson in 1912. Such resistance meant that, by the time of the war, matters remained unresolved. Both Protestants and Catholics from across the island fought alongside empire troops in France and on the other fronts of the war.[31]

By Easter 1916, however, frustrations amongst more radical nationalist elements in the south of the island had grown to boiling point. Taking advantage of the British attention elsewhere, around 1,600 men in Dublin took over key government buildings, including the Post Office on O'Connell Street, in what was called the Easter Rising. From there, one of the rebel leaders, Patrick Pearse, issued his proclamation on behalf of the Provisional Government of the Irish Republic. The British soon rallied from their surprise, however, and within a week the Rising had been suppressed, with 450 of the rebel volunteers killed. The British took their revenge upon the rebel leadership, executing them shortly afterwards in Kilmainham prison. The unquestioning severity of this treatment led to an increasing nationalist dissent in the succeeding years, led by Sinn Fein, which had been established in 1904 by Arthur Griffith.

After election success in 1919, Sinn Fein proclaimed a breakaway national assembly in Dublin, with Eamon de Valera as President. There followed over a year of guerrilla war between what was later to become the Irish Republican Army and the occupying British, in which hundreds died. The attacks on the British met with a brutal response, particularly from the notorious Black and Tans, an auxiliary police force. After splitting away the six counties of the predominantly Protestant north of the island in 1920, the British signed a treaty in 1921 establishing the Irish Free State. Fighting broke out between nationalists holding differing ideals about the agreed compromise, resulting in civil war, in which the pro-treaty forces led by Michael Collins fought against De Valera's anti-treaty Sinn Fein. The pro-treaty force eventually won out (although Collins had been ambushed and killed), and William Cosgrove put together a government for the Free State which finally came into being in 1922.

These events form a backdrop to the discussion of nationalism in James Joyce's work, which will appear in Chapter 5. But the immediate chronicler of these struggles in Ireland was W. B. Yeats. His elegy 'Easter 1916', which commemorates the transformation wrought upon the rebels both by their place in this event, and by the event within history itself, was eventually collected in *Michael Robartes and the Dancer* in 1920. It appeared there alongside 'Sixteen Dead Men', 'The Rose Tree', and 'On a Political Prisoner' (to his friend and imprisoned rebel Countess Markievicz), all puzzling through what had happened on April 1916. As 'Sixteen Dead Men' shows in its opening lines, these events show Yeats hardening against circumstance: 'O but we talked at large before / The sixteen men were shot . . .'.[32] But *Michael Robartes* taken as a whole also sets the events surrounding the Rising in the light of Yeats's move in the latter part of the 1910s towards an eclectic and personal visionary model of history and mythology. This was a model in which such events can be perceived as part of the movement of larger forces.

This vision of a recurring pattern to history is most noticeable in the apocalyptic poem 'The Second Coming', written by Yeats in January 1919. Reviewing the troubles in Ireland alongside the First World War and the 1917 Russian Revolution, the poem proclaims that 'Things fall apart; the centre cannot hold; / Mere anarchy is loosed upon the world'. In desperation, the speaker looks for a sign, 'Surely some revelation is at hand'. But the image that comes, rather than offering a vision of salvation, 'troubles my sight'. It is a dreadful compounding of Christ's prophecy of his resurrection with a devastating beast from the biblical Book of Revelation into a nightmare: 'And what rough beast, its hour come round at last, / Slouches towards Bethlehem to be born?' (p. 187).

Yeats's subsequent collection, *The Tower* (1928), concedes once more the direct pressure of historical circumstance upon the visionary potential of the poetry. It contains poems reflecting upon the struggle with the Black and Tans ('Nineteen Hundred and Nineteen') and the events of the early 1920s that took place near Yeats's home, Thoor Ballylee ('Meditations in Time of Civil War'). What is most noticeable, however, in this work, is the continued and precarious movement towards a world of allusion and visionary symbolism private to Yeats himself. Such a world would provide a means of resisting the growing murderousness of the real world. This, combined with Yeats's own ageing, brings about a retreat into magisterially orchestrated dreams of beauty and permanence, a late re-inflection of his earlier Symbolism. So, for example, 'Sailing to Byzantium', a 1926 poem set at the start of *The Tower*, begins by confirming his sense that his country, Ireland, 'is no country for old men'. Instead, he must move away from history and natural fertility into the enduring world of art and artifice, the supreme idealization of early Byzantium (p. 194):

> Once out of nature I shall never take
> My bodily form from any natural thing,
> But such a form as Grecian goldsmiths make
> Of hammered gold and gold enamelling . . .

The escape seems carried by the momentum of the rhyme and syntax. But the whole structure of the magnificent poetry, which matches the 'sensual music' he seeks in his ideal world, is falsely predicated on that initial 'Once'.

It is, of course, impossible to so escape the world except through imagining a place like Byzantium. The dream of eternity through art is registered as impractical even as it is most beautifully rendered. In later Yeats, therefore, we find his grasp of the brutal realities of the post-civil-war world in balance with imaginative encounters with history and mythology. The realities bring a new note to the kinds of cultural and historical retrieval which had always formed a part of what Eliot called Yeats's (and Joyce's) 'mythical method'. I shall go on to consider in the next chapter the origins and contexts of that method, as they impact upon modernist writing generally.

Notes

1 Hew Strachan, *The First World War,* vol. I: *To Arms* (Oxford, 2001), pp. 1000, 1005ff. Sigmund Freud's observation of war neuroses partly led him to introduce a new theory of competing drives in the human psyche in his book *Beyond the Pleasure Principle* (1920). He re-configured his earlier map of the mind into one which prioritized the opposition between Eros, the love instinct, and Thanatos, the death instinct.
2 See Trudi Tate, *Modernism, History, and the First World War* (Manchester, 1998), Chapter 5, 'The Tank and the Manufacture of Consent'.
3 Wyndham Lewis, *Blasting and Bombardiering* (London, 1982), p. 114.
4 Edmund Blunden, *Undertones of War* (Harmondsworth, 1982), p. 7.
5 James Joll, *Europe: An International History* (London, 1990), p. 239.
6 *The Letters of T. S. Eliot,* vol. I: *1898–1922,* edited by Valerie Eliot (London, 1988), p. 230.
7 *Selected Prose of T. S. Eliot,* edited by Frank Kermode (London, 1975), pp. 63, 177.
8 Ezra Pound, *Personae,* edited by Lea Baechler and A. Walton Litz (New York, 1990), pp. 185–95.
9 *Blast 1* (Santa Rosa, 1997 reprint), p. 30.
10 Ezra Pound, *Gaudier-Brzeska: A Memoir* (New York, 1970), p. 92.
11 'Anthem for Doomed Youth', in *The Poems of Wilfred Owen,* edited by Jon Stallworthy (London, 1990), p. 76.
12 Siegfried Sassoon, *The War Poems,* edited by Rupert Hart-Davis (London, 1999), p. 21.
13 A similar contrast haunts Richard Aldington's Imagist poems from the trenches such as 'Insouciance' and 'Living Sepulchres'. See *Imagist Poetry,* edited by Peter Jones (Harmondsworth, 1972), p. 57.
14 *The Penguin Book of First World War Poetry,* edited by Jon Silkin (Harmondsworth, 1979), p. 81.
15 During the war, the British government established a Department of Information, which included News, Cinema, and Political Intelligence Divisions, in order to circulate anti-German propaganda and patriotic stories. Many of these were false stories (including the suggestion that the Germans had established factories to melt down British soldiers' corpses to make candles), which, particularly early in the war, had a dramatic effect on recruitment figures for the army.
16 Rebecca West, *The Return of the Soldier* (London, 1980), p. 16.

17 D. H. Lawrence, *Lady Chatterley's Lover*, edited by Michael Squires (Harmondsworth, 2000), pp. 42, 44.

18 Jose Harris, *Private Lives, Public Spirit: Britain 1870–1914* (Harmondsworth, 1994), p. 20.

19 D. H. Lawrence, *Kangaroo*, edited by Bruce Steele (Harmondsworth, 1997), p. 216.

20 Arthur Marwick, *The Deluge: British Society and the First World War* (London, 1965), pp. 136–7.

21 *The Collected Letters of D. H. Lawrence*, edited by Harry T. Moore (London, 1962), vol. I, p. 366.

22 D. H. Lawrence, *Women in Love*, edited by Charles Ross (Harmondsworth, 1986), pp. 207–8.

23 There is a similar attempt to articulate a new kind of relation between the sexes made by Virginia Woolf in the novel she was working on in the latter period of the war, *Night and Day*. In the tortuous courtship between Katherine Hilbery and Ralph Denham, Woolf perceives a challenge to the normalized rituals of marriage between social equals which previsions *Lady Chatterley's Lover*.

24 Lawrence had read Nietzsche's work by early 1910, when he borrowed it from the public library in Croydon, where he was then employed as a school teacher. See John Worthen, *D. H. Lawrence: The Early Years 1885–1912* (Cambridge, 1991), pp. 210–12.

25 Ford Madox Ford, *Parade's End* (London, 1992), p. 113.

26 Ford Madox Ford, *The Good Soldier* (London, 1991), p. 22.

27 Richard Aldington, *Death of a Hero* (London, 1965), p. 226.

28 Marwick, *The Deluge*, pp. 109–11.

29 Many of the jobs in factories were taken back by men returning from the Front in 1918. But a trend had been established which would see more than three-quarters of a million more women in paid employment by 1930 than there had been before the war, with resultant shifts in social and sexual relations. John Stevenson, *British Society 1914–45* (Harmondsworth, 1990), pp. 83–5, 169–70.

30 D. H. Lawrence, *The Complete Short Novels*, edited by Keith Sagar and Melissa Partridge (Harmondsworth, 1990), pp. 173, 205.

31 John Davis, *A History of Britain, 1885–1939* (Basingstoke, 1999), pp. 94–6.

32 W. B. Yeats, *Collected Poems*, edited by Richard J. Finneran (Basingstoke, 1983), p. 182.

|4|

Modernism and primitivism

Extract 3 on pp. 142–3 is taken from the 1920 book, *Instinct and the Unconscious*, by the doctor, psychiatrist, and ethnologist (student of human racial characteristics), W. H. R. Rivers. Famously, Rivers was amongst those to treat the soldier-poets from the First World War Siegfried Sassoon and Wilfred Owen, when each was temporarily invalided out of the army and taken to Craiglockhart War Hospital, near Edinburgh in Scotland, for treatment. *Instinct and the Unconscious* contains Rivers's reflections on his treatment of many shell-shock victims at the hospital, and pursues an argument with the presumption by the psychoanalyst Sigmund Freud that adult neuroses are caused by childhood sexual traumas. Rivers counters Freud's central premise by holding instead that the First World War, and the mass trauma it caused, had proved that there was a deeper-seated instinct, which was under threat in these circumstances, the instinct for self-preservation. Rivers is fascinated by the ways in which that instinct is something humans share with birds and animals, and that many human responses, such as cowering or shaking with fear when threatened, are shared with the animal world.

The extract (pp. 142–3) derives from a wartime article Rivers included as an appendix to *Instinct and the Unconscious*. 'The Instinct of Acquisition', considering humans' desire for land possession, is obviously pertinent to the aggressive territorial manoeuvrings of the war. Yet, in considering this instinct, Rivers typically draws upon his earlier comparative studies of different races, and especially the 'savage' Melanesians, about whom he had written a famous book. Rivers's weighing of the 'primitive' and the 'modern' (not always to the advantage of the latter, as you can see) is characteristic, as this chapter will reveal, of various intellectual and literary considerations at this time. His counterpoising of Melanesians and birds seems at first precariously dismissive and racist. But, as the end of the extract shows, this is determined by his further interest in the 'evolution of societies' as they are determined by 'general psychological laws'. Rivers's ethnological and psychiatric interests come together, in other words, when considering the instincts behind the war and also the traumas suffered by its combatants. This weighing of ancient and modern, the determination to look beyond history into myth and the universal human psyche for a sense of meaning and purpose in the contemporary 'waste land', was typical at the time, and informs many of the major modernist texts under discussion in this book.

Anthropology and religion

As the opening chapter of this book has argued, one of the definitive aspects of modernism was the way in which modernist writers sought a variety of strategies to resolve a shared attention to historical degeneration or crisis. Certain of these strategies involved the appropriation by artists of non-contemporary, and often non-European, models and stories that provided them with a distinctive means of structuring their work at a time of perceived contemporary historical crisis. These were models derived from a range of sources: literary ones, in the case of the recourse to Greek mythologies by such as Joyce and Pound (to be discussed below), or in Pound's interest in Chinese literature and philosophy, or (with Yeats) in the Japanese Noh; but there were also models drawn more immediately from the processes of recent imperial expansion.

The late nineteenth century had seen the major European powers, Britain, France, and Germany, extending their hold over West Africa. In the process, significant artefacts, religious totems, and artworks were looted from supposedly uncultured peoples, such as those from Benin and from Asanteland. These artworks soon found their way into metropolitan museums and art-house boutiques in Europe, where they had a crucial impact upon a range of painters and writers who were seeking to recon-figure their art towards the changed conditions of the modern world. Pablo Picasso's early interest in ancient masks from his native Spain was expanded on a visit to the Ethnographical Museum in Paris in 1907, where he saw African tribal art. These models moved his work forward significantly towards his Cubist phase, and altered Western artists' sense of perspective forever. In the 'Totem' chapter of D. H. Lawrence's novel *Women in Love* (1920), there is a debate over the nature of an African statue of a woman taken to be in labour. The debate leads the central figure, Rupert Birkin, to begin to develop his ideas – even if hesitantly and patriarchally – about 'culture in the physical consciousness' which crucially inform the book's attempts to define a new kind of relationship between the sexes.[1]

At the same time as these immediate cultural impacts of colonial contact were being felt in the imperial capitals, there was from the 1890s through to the First World War and beyond an increasing intellectual interest in ancient world cultures and so-called primitive peoples. This interest brought together the kinds of ethnography being carried out in Africa with the 'scientific' study of the rituals and practices of early mankind, which had been developing across the nineteenth century in the work of European anthropologists and religious historians. Works like Leo Frobenius's *The Voice of Africa* (which was translated into English in 1913), a study of the Yoruba people, were assimilated into modernist thinking after the war. Lawrence read the book in 1918, and it clearly influenced his later writings on primitive ritual in stories like 'The Woman Who Rode Away' (1924) and in his novel *The Plumed Serpent* (1926). Ezra Pound read Frobenius avidly in the late 1920s, and the ethnographer's theories about art emerging as an expression of a primitive racial purity had a dubious influence upon Pound's politics and attraction towards Fascism in the 1930s.

For the English-speaking world, the anthropological strand in nineteenth-century thought culminated in the start of publication in 1890 of *The Golden Bough: A Study in Magic and Religion* (it eventually ran to twelve volumes and publication of the last was in 1915). This huge work by the Cambridge ethnologist Sir James G. Frazer, which sought to understand the nature of the priesthood to the goddess Diana in ancient Italy, had a profound impact upon modernist thought. In the prefatory paragraph to his notes on *The Waste Land* (1922), T. S. Eliot proclaimed the general indebtedness of his poem to Frazer's study, 'which has influenced our generation profoundly'. Eliot kept himself aware of these ideas through his reading of subsequent debates about the nature of early religion in works like Emile Durkheim's *The Elementary Forms of Religious Life*, translated in 1912. But, when famously formulating his 'mythical method' for modern writing, in response to James Joyce's *Ulysses* in the essay of 1923, it is *The Golden Bough* which is again singled out by Eliot as the exemplar of that method in anthropological thought.

In other emerging fields of intellectual and scientific enquiry at the time, Frazer's work was also taken as key. Sigmund Freud, himself an avid collector of 'pre-historic' art who had sculptures from the Near East in his consulting room, published *Totem and Taboo* in 1913. The work draws heavily upon *The Golden Bough* and Frazer's subsequent work on *Totemism and Exogamy* (1910). Freud's argument that primitive drives towards religion, sacrifice, and magic or animism underlie many modern ills regalvanizes, just before the First World War, the sense that underneath the contemporary mind a whole realm of ancient ritual, killing, and belief waits to break through to the surface. The essential element of Frazer's study for many writers in the early twentieth century was the way in which it provided a stratified map of the phases of development in human psychology and civilization which, at the same time, also recognized the uncertainties surrounding all such endeavours.

Frazer's map relies upon Darwinian evolutionary ideas, in that for him humankind has moved through three distinct, and progressively more developed and sophisticated, phases. He emphasizes the universality of humanity – 'the essential similarity of man's chief wants everywhere and at all times' – at the same time as he stresses the way in which history shows it to be adaptable and changeable. Man has moved, he claims, from an age dominated by magic, through religion, to the current scientific age. The age of magic was founded upon belief in individual strength and in 'a certain established order of nature'. Once, however, that belief in an individual's ability to understand and control nature is proved imaginary, humanity throws itself 'humbly on certain great invisible beings behind the veil of nature'. This again proved illusory, however, with the understanding 'that the succession of natural events is not determined by immutable laws', and so humanity switched to its latest phase of intellectual ambition, the age of science.

At the end of his monumental enquiry, however, Frazer acknowledges that, despite his having carefully categorized vast amounts of mythology and literature under his three phases, this might not be the end of the story, or even the right story at all. The scientific age is itself only one moment in the 'advance of knowledge', which 'is an infinite progression towards a goal that for ever recedes'. The virtue of Frazer's ambitious project for contemporary thinking is that it established the potentially cyclical continuities between all its modes of understanding, from magic through religion to science, and back again. As he says in conclusion, 'the dreams of magic may one day be the waking realities of science'.[2] Christianity, for instance, is seen by Frazer as a phase in the development of religious practice which has links back to the various myths about seasonal change and vegetation from the most ancient times. But it is also, in Frazer's developmental model, becoming superseded by other forms of relation to the broader 'cosmos', something that appealed to the increasingly sceptical world in the early twentieth century.[3] Most telling, perhaps (and hence its appeal for Freud), is Frazer's presumption that tribal and cultural religious and artistic practice, through imagery and mythology, bears echoes in the individual psyche, and that the primitive instinct for ritual and magic resides within everyone.

The impact on literary work of Frazer's model is both felt directly through allusion to his work, and instilled more generally in this era. It perhaps gained added resonance in the years after the First World War, which appeared to have returned humankind to its presumed innate savagery. The structure of *The Waste Land*, however tenuous and difficult to perceive, certainly partakes of the key ideas developed by Frazer, as Eliot acknowledges. The uncertain intimations of the coming of water to bring a new fertility to the land, and the vegetation ceremony referred to in Part V of the sequence, closely follow both the particularities of Frazer's discussion of vegetation myth and ritual and his more general cyclical model of civilization. The inclusion within this context of a reference to Christ's appearance after the crucifixion at line 359, 'who is the third who walks always beside you?', conforms with Frazer's argument that Christianity proposed a development of these ancient practices. Recurrent passages revealing psychological trauma and breakdown across the poem reflect Frazer's concluding awareness that a 'dark shadow' lies across his 'scientific' model of human progress, and his new alertness to its link to the primitive origins of magic. This is the shadow of the fact that 'great forces . . . seem to be making silently but relentlessly for the destruction of this starry universe'. Yeats's visionary poems like 'The Second Coming' will offer a similar reading of this historical phase, and its inverted Christianity. But Frazer's immediate alertness here is to the late nineteenth century's fear of entropy, the sense that the universe is failing and the sun dying. He is also attentive to the fact that science itself is beginning to fail in its understanding of potentially destructive powers, operating both from without and within the human consciousness.

In the common climate of fear and degeneration, the aspect of Frazer's work which seems to have become generally celebrated by modernism is that in which the primitive and its alliance with nature, ritual (including sacrifice), and magic operates within modern consciousness. This is so, even as the primitive is seen to work also to question modern beliefs in develop-ment and sophistication. 'The Art-Instinct is Always Primitive' proclaims the 'Manifesto' of 'Vorticism' signed up to by several artists in June 1914, in Wyndham Lewis's magazine *Blast*.[4] In other works, both earlier and later in the period, that primitivism takes on a complex and shifting status in con-nection both with the text in which it appears, and in that text's diagnosis of the modern world.

In Conrad's *Heart of Darkness*, we recall, Marlow's knowledge of the destructiveness and insanity of the imperial enterprise in Africa leads his thoughts, and the attention of his audience, to the history which lies beneath the contemporary streets of the city of London. 'And this also . . . has been one of the dark places of the earth', he says.[5] Such interruptive moments and speculations recur frequently within modernist texts, as a further aspect of their multiple layering of seemingly diverse materials. Virginia Woolf's *Mrs Dalloway* (1925) is punctuated by moments in which Conrad's crucial text seems to reside just beneath the surface of Woolf's own words. On seeing the agitated and strange actions of the shell-shocked victim of World War One Septimus Smith, for instance, a nameless woman, who has herself left her family home and is adrift in the city streets, wants to cry out 'Horror! Horror!' Her urge is a clear echo of the 'insight' attained by Conrad's Kurtz through his brutal exploitation of the native population and contortion of imperialist ambition.[6] At a later moment in the book, however, Peter Walsh, the disillusioned friend of Mrs Dalloway's who has wasted his life in the colonial service in India, hears a sound as he walks through the streets near Regent's Park tube station. The sound is that of a seemingly androgynous (but actually female) singer begging for money, 'the voice of no age or sex, the voice of an ancient spring spouting from the earth' (pp. 106–7):

> Through all ages – when the pavement was grass, when it was swamp, through the age of tusk and mammoth, through the age of silent sunrise – the battered woman . . . stood singing of love . . . As the ancient song bubbled up opposite Regent's Park Tube Station, still the earth seemed green and flowery.

This is an odd moment in the book; Peter Walsh has just come to understand that he himself has been in love with, and perhaps is now loved by, Clarissa Dalloway. The song is to that extent confirmation of a reality sadly lost to him. But, in another way, it also strips away the surface of the modern city to reveal a more 'primitive' truth. Woolf is often preoccupied by this intersection of the ancient and the modern, or by the way in which the modern (as in Joyce's sense) ironically debases the reality of older meanings. In her previous novel, *Jacob's Room* (1922), she focuses on the primitive, Celtic, actuality beneath the modern surface of the English county of Cornwall:

> These white Cornish cottages are built on the edge of the cliff; the garden grows gorse more readily than cabbages; and for hedge, some primeval man has piled granite boulders. In one of these, to hold, an historian conjectures, the victim's blood, a basin has been hollowed, but in our time it serves more tamely to seat those tourists who wish for an uninterrupted view of the Gurnard's Head.[7]

Woolf's tone is mocking yet edgy. Before the tourists' gaze, the woman of one cottage, Mrs Pascoe, becomes simply a kitsch example of a former way of life: 'Look – she has to draw water from a well in the garden.' Woolf's prose at this point becomes inflected by the language of the tourist's guide-book, if not an academic treatise ('an historian conjectures'). The 'primeval' nature of the landscape becomes assimilated to that hollow view, its puta-tively ancient rites part of the glamour and redundancy of the world-weary modern trail. Yet, once the tourists staring at the cottage have wandered on to their next sights, Mrs Pascoe is seen rather differently through the prose, as she stares at the sea, 'for the millionth time, perhaps'. She is 'hard, wise, wholesome . . . signifying in a room full of sophisticated people the flesh and blood of life' (p. 44).

That 'flesh and blood', of course, chimes back to the blood alluded to just earlier, associated with 'primeval man' and worship. As with the 'ancient song' in the modern London street in *Mrs Dalloway*, the writing hovers self-consciously yet confirmingly around the sense that there is a more primitive truth underlying the surfaces of modern life. There is genuineness and honesty, which defies 'sophisticated' attempts to manage and understand it (Mrs Pascoe 'would tell a lie, though, as soon as the truth'). To this extent, Woolf shares in a contemporary fascination with versions of the 'uncivilized' or the 'primitive' which were current in modern art at the time. The Post-Impressionist paintings, which powerfully affected Woolf when she first saw them at the exhibitions of 1910 and 1912 organized by Roger Fry, included work such as the Tahiti pictures of Paul Gauguin. This was work fascinated by the 'primitive' beauty and unashamed sexuality of the South Sea islanders (Woolf caused a scandal at the Post-Impressionist Ball linked to the first exhibition, when she and her sister appeared as 'Gauguin girls'). The shock impact of these pictures brought a conservative reaction from the intellec-tual and journalistic establishment in Britain against their 'pornographic' nature, and against the fact that they seemed 'the work of madmen'.[8]

Woolf, like many other members of the artistic avant-garde in Paris and London, was also excited by the tours in 1911 and 1913 by the dance company Ballets Russes, choreographed by Sergei Diaghilev and headed by Vaslav Nijinsky. The Ballets Russes offered dance to new music by the French composer Claude Debussy but, most notoriously, by the Russian Igor Stravinsky. Stravinsky's deployment of fairytale and folklore, from his first ballet score *The Firebird* to *Petrushka* (given in London, 1911) and *Le Sacre du printemps (The Rite of Spring*, 1913), encouraged a departure from earlier musical conventions in its use of harsh rhythmic patterns, chromaticism, and dissonance. *Le Sacre* caused riots amongst its early audiences because of its radicalism. Its 'scenes of pagan Russia' pictured orgiastic violence with crashing orchestration. The story of the ballet, in which a virgin is sacrificed to the land in order to encourage fertility in the crops, refers once again to an ancient blood rite, as did *The Golden Bough*, or, glancingly, the passage in *Jacob's Room* on Cornwall. Mrs Pascoe's 'flesh and blood' nature is a further variation upon an established version of European cosmopolitan modernity, in a narrative moment nostalgic for imaginary pre-Christian worlds.

Related imaginary worlds became the object of the various quests undertaken in D. H. Lawrence's later works. *Kangaroo* (1923), the novel of ideas in which Lawrence's struggle to understand the European wartime experience challenges traditional form, sets his experience against the possibilities contained in the 'newest country', Australia. At one point early on in the book, the Lawrence alter ego in the novel, Richard Somers, wanders out from Sydney into the Australian bush:

> He walked on . . . and had just come to a clump of tall, nude dead trees, shining almost phosphorescent with the moon, when the terror of the bush overcame him . . . And now, there was something among the trees, and his hair began to stir with terror, on his head. There was a presence . . . He knew quite well it was nothing . . . But his spine ran cold like ice.

This 'spirit of the place', a sense of the 'phantom-like' aboriginal vastness and of the continent, challenges Somers's preconceptions about the new and freer life to be obtained in the escape from Europe. Instead, he flirts with the extremist politics of a radical group headed by the man named Kangaroo, and falls into disillusion and despair. The novel ends with him simply moving on and away, the experience in the bush seemingly having rendered all idealism irrelevant.

Lawrence's next novel, set now in Mexico, *The Plumed Serpent* (1926), finds him preoccupied by similar issues. Kate Leslie is the Irish widow of a nationalist leader in her own country. In Mexico she finds herself increasingly drawn towards a religious sect and its leaders, whose aim is to eradicate from the country the Christian God, who had been imposed upon it through Spanish colonization, and to restore the primitive Mexican gods. Vast tracts of the book are taken up with Lawrence's invented rituals for the worship of Quetzalcoatl, and with the hymns sung to him. The author clearly seeks, in other words, to draw his readers into a proximate understanding of the possibilities revealed to Kate, who undergoes a mystical marriage to one of the leaders, Don Cipriano. Kate is reluctant to join in and to believe all of this, largely because of her sense of her independence and of her gender. 'It was wonderful . . . But where was woman, in this terrible interchange . . .?'

The novel ends with her submitting to what is going on, partly because of her attraction to Cipriano, partly because she sees in the rituals developed

for the cult an echo of those savage forces which challenge Western consciousness and civilization the world over. As Cipriano and his associates
prepare to remove the Catholic icons from a village church, in order to
replace them with their own,

> the sound that always made her heart stand still woke on the invisible
> air. It was the sound of drums, of tom-toms rapidly beaten. The same
> sound she had heard in the distance, in the tropical dusk of Ceylon,
> from the temple at sunset. The sound she had heard from the edge of
> the forest in the north . . . The sound that wakes dark, ancient echoes
> in the heart of every man, the thud of the primeval world.[9]

In the terms of the contemporary ethnography with which Lawrence was
familiar, Kate's experience in Mexico enables her to reconnect her modern
sophisticated consciousness with her magical and ritual nature. The novel
maps thoroughly the difficulties in doing so, but the ambition of the work is
typical of the urge to measure the present against the imagined ancient past,
which is characteristic of modernist writing.

Empire

The early years of the modernist period marked the high point of the British
Empire in a literal sense. This was the moment at which it attained its
greatest expanse of territory and seemed to have embraced the greatest
number of peoples. And yet, as multi-layered texts like Joseph Conrad's
Almayer's Folly and *Heart of Darkness* reveal, that sense of colonial
assurance went alongside feelings of uncertainty about the imperial project.
There were doubts expressed about its brutal effects upon colonized native
peoples, and about the deleterious effect it was also having upon the minds
of those involved in following through colonial ambition and enterprise.
The popular apologist for the British Empire, Rudyard Kipling, had, a few
years before Conrad's novella appeared, encapsulated these qualms in his
1897 poem 'Recessional', where he expresses his fears that imperialism has
gone out of control as everyone has become 'drunk with the sight of power':

> Far-called, our navies melt away;
>   On dune and headland sinks the fire:
> Lo, all our pomp of yesterday
>   Is one with Nineveh and Tyre!
> Judge of the Nations, spare us yet,
> Lest we forget – lest we forget![10]

Kipling's fear in the poem as elsewhere is that the idealism which originally impelled the imperial adventure, the bringing of commerce, 'civilization', and Christianity to 'heathen' peoples, is beginning to withdraw. Duty and Law, those primal virtues of British nationhood, might be forgotten. A recessional, which gives the poem its title, is a hymn sung in church whilst the clergy and choir withdraw at the end of the service. With the extension of the empire further and further from its centre in London there comes a weakening of that idealism. This was, of course, to prove a true warning with the advent of the Anglo-Boer War from 1899 to 1902, when the British army was held at bay by a small band of rebel farmers. Kipling fears and warns that, with its extended power, the empire is itself paradoxically becoming redundant, one with the destroyed ancient kingdoms of Nineveh and Tyre. More to the point, he fears that God ('Judge of the Nations') must be merciful towards believers at this moment, since, in the turmoil of such colonial expansion, He seems in danger of being forgotten.

Related to this is Kipling's extraordinary fear that the colonial project will unleash an unpredictable result, that 'we loose / Wild tongues that have not Thee in awe, / Such boastings as the Gentiles use, / Or lesser breeds without the Law'. Kipling's lines are freighted with prejudice ('lesser breeds') against the non-believers or Gentiles. But they are also fraught with nightmare that the British project of bringing enlightenment to those nations and peoples in 'darkness' might free them into an articulation which is then turned back against the colonizers. The dread is that these newly defiant voices will be used for unpredictable purposes, including a disavowal of the Christian God.[11] The decorum of the English language itself, so integral to the civilization and to the religious conversion which the empire was seeking to achieve, might become distorted and even uncontrollable ('Wild'). The colonial encounter, the project whereby the height of human attainment in the English culture and language is brought into contact with those who worship the 'reeking tube and iron shard', might end by undermining the very bases of 'power'.

Some of the 'wild' exuberance of modernist writing (as I will explore further in Chapter 5 below) indeed emerged in countries that perceived themselves to have recently emerged from British colonial domination (America), or which were undergoing a period of dissent to that domination (Ireland). That exuberance often derives from its ironical 'take' upon the very concern Kipling voiced in 'Recessional'. The 'wildness' of the native tongue in its use of English gained through colonial encounter, when seen from the perspective of the colonized themselves, is actually conceived as having a richness and strength unavailable to the English themselves. These tensions are captured best, and most iconically, through their impact upon subsequent writing from Ireland – in James Joyce's staging of a debate between the emerging writer Stephen Dedalus and his university tutor in *A Portrait of the Artist as a Young Man* (1916).

Stephen's Dean of Studies is an Englishman, a convert to the religion in which Stephen has been raised, Catholicism. Whilst seeking to illustrate for Stephen a fine point of theology, the Dean talks about the funnel he is holding, which was at that time used to pour oil into a lamp to fuel light.

> – That? said Stephen. Is that called a funnel? Is it not a tundish?
> – What is a tundish?
> – That. The . . . the funnel.
> – Is that called a tundish in Ireland? asked the dean. I never heard the word in my life.
> – It is called a tundish in Lower Drumcondra, said Stephen laughing, where they speak the best English.[12]

The suburb of the city of Dublin where the Dedalus family lives speaks a different version of the colonizer's language to that of the Englishman himself, and yet it is in Stephen's estimation 'the best English'. The irony of the situation is that 'tundish' was in fact a current word for such funnels in the English spoken by the Elizabethans who, in the sixteenth century, carried out comprehensive colonization of Ireland. In this exchange, therefore, we witness an exact rendition of the process of forgetting Kipling so feared, a sense that the English language will lose sight of its past and also set loose a seeming wildness which challenges the authority of the imperialist's discourse. Stephen, as emerging writer, is therefore caught in a paradoxical awareness that he is subject to the impositions of the colonial language itself ('My soul frets in the shadow of his language') but is also thereby challenged and freed or licensed to seek to evade all such entrapments, partly by the unconscious centrality of his own idiom (p. 220).

Stephen's (and Joyce's) urgency in defining a national conscience and a distinctive aesthetic under these circumstances is further exacerbated throughout the novel by the sense that the language has become debased by the interrelated forces not only of imperialism, but also of modern mercantilism and capitalism.[13] His attempts to express his ideas and ideals frequently include a sense that 'the use of the word in the marketplace is quite different' or that a crucial term for him like 'beauty' 'in the market-place . . . has another sense' (pp. 203, 231). In other words, for those in all metropolitan centres from Dublin to London, Paris, and New York modernity and commerce threatened the ambition to conceive of an art and an aesthetics that was adequate to its demands.

Joseph Conrad's fiction from early to late had been preoccupied by the way in which imperialism and trade combined to create the destruction not just of native customs and ideals, but also the souls of those Westerners involved in the enterprise. These preoccupations sharpened in his later, more allegorical work, which views life in the colonies through a variety of literary modes, including tragi-comedy and romance. At the centre of his vision of colonial life, however, remains his deep sense of the void and the purposelessness of the European enterprise of expanding into other lands. Kurtz's mad success in garnering titanic amounts of ivory is the extreme early rendition of this by Conrad. In the later *Victory* (1915), the story echoes facets of Shakespeare's late play *The Tempest*, as the central figure, the Prospero-like drifter Axel Heyst, retreats to a remote island in the Malayan archipelago with a Miranda figure, the young English girl Lena. The plot then shifts towards comedy, as Heyst is rumoured to have hidden on his island a vast store of gold. The novel is largely taken up, as a result, with the grotesque, even cartoonic, attempts of Ricardo, Mr Jones and the Caliban-like Pedro to steal the 'gold' away. In the process, Lena is accidentally killed and Heyst commits suicide in misery.

In its use of ambiguous symbolism (does the gold exist and does the plot have value and meaning, or not?) and in its literariness, *Victory* looks back to Conrad's earlier masterpiece, *Nostromo* (1904), a work which again focused upon the dubious riches to be obtained through exploitation of a colonial space. There, Charles Gould finds the silver from his mine under threat, once the mythical country of Sulaco erupts into civil war. He acquiesces in a plan put forward by the trusted but opportunistic Italian Nostromo (known as 'our man' by the white population), and the nihilistic journalist Decoud, to send the silver to safety in a small boat. The boat is, however, damaged by a rebel ship as it sails out into the gulf, and Nostromo and Decoud hide the silver ingots on some small islands, the Isabels. After Decoud's suicide in despair at the failure of the plan and the deceit he has practised, and after peace has been restored to Sulaco, Nostromo makes secret trips to the island to lay hands on some of the hidden silver. He continues the pretence that it was lost in the collision in the gulf. On one of his journeys, though, he is shot and killed by the lighthouse keeper on the island, with whose daughter he has fallen in love.

As even this brief précis of the two novels demonstrates, however, in his later work Conrad presented through his stories of the colonies a consistently fatalistic vision of modernity. The 'riches' presumed to have been acquired through the colonial enterprise in these situations are either non-existent (although they cause the deaths of the protagonists), or useless (Nostromo's inability to enjoy his ill-gotten gains). The corruptibility of even the 'heroic' figures in these books, like Nostromo, and the farcical/tragic fate of dreamers such as Heyst, enforce a sense that in the colonial context Europeans are uncertain and divided, sometimes even against their own best interests. As indicated, Conrad's literary forms in these instances are equally mixed and unstable. Both *Victory* and *Nostromo*, like earlier novels such as *Lord Jim* (1900), contain strong elements of popular romance. They all contain an adventure story and are novels of action suited to the genre of imperial exploits. And yet, at the same time, many of these elements fail to connect and resolve themselves with each other. The seemingly random and absurd deaths of Nostromo and Lena underline the dramatic but hollow conclusions ('The horror! The horror!') of the imperial encounter, and confirm Conrad's modernist vision.

That vision finds its resonance in other works staging similar encounters between the English and other populations at this time. E. M. Forster's early novels had shown him intrigued by the way in which parochial and socially repressed English people could have their habits and ideals challenged by their experiences whilst on holiday on the continent, and in Italy in particular. Lucy, in *A Room With a View* (1908), for example, witnesses a riot and death in the city of Florence:

> The well-known world had broken up, and there emerged Florence, a magic city where people thought and did the most extraordinary things ... Was there more in her frank beauty than met the eye – the power, perhaps, to evoke passions, good and bad, and to bring them speedily to a fulfilment?[14]

The answer to this question is, of course, 'yes', as Lucy falls for George Emerson. She spends the rest of the novel struggling in her conscience between her duty towards her vapid fiancé Cecil Vyse, and her duty to herself to remember 'the experiences of her own heart', which she finally does on the last page. It is when Forster considers these issues in the context of his own experience of India, which he does in *A Passage to India* (1924), that the novel treating them moves beyond a situation of painful social comedy into something more complex. *A Passage to India*'s reading of the late imperial situation is one which suggests that attempts to achieve spiritual and legal understanding between peoples bring severe damage and, within a continuing situation of inequality, only ends in textual, religious, and racial confusion.

At the start of the novel, Forster establishes several divergent responses to India – responses partly divided on gender lines. The white British colonial administrators are resistant to any notion that they should seek to understand the culture and the customs of the people they rule. The land and its people intrigue Mrs Moore and Adela Quested, who is in the country to establish whether she will marry Mrs Moore's son Ronny. Further potential for breaking through boundaries is embodied in the sexually ambiguous figure of Fielding, head of the Government College, who moves between the two cultures, not least through his close friendship with a Muslim, Dr Aziz.

Mrs Moore's accidental contact with Aziz, when they encounter one another in a moonlit mosque, sees his initially aggressive proprietorship over his native religion shift into a friendly dialogue of mutual respect. This seems to suggest the possibility of true connection between British and Indians, if only between the more eccentric and complex members of each race. But the ambiguous moment in the Marabar Caves, when Adela Quested believes, if only for a time, that she has been molested sexually by Aziz, throws relations between both the communities in Chandrapore into polarized distrust. The very setting of the Marabar, and the intense heat of the day, overturn Mrs Moore's sense of religious possibility to be discovered in India ('God is here', she had chided Aziz in the mosque):

> The crush and the smells she could forget, but the echo began in some indescribable way to undermine her hold on life. Coming at a moment when she chanced to be fatigued, it had managed to murmur: 'Pathos, piety, courage – they exist, but are identical, and so is filth. Everything exists, nothing has value.'[15]

Like the Australian bush to Lawrence's Somers, the Marabar becomes a kind of waste land for Mrs Moore. It echoes with a voice of primitive instinct and ritual that challenges her hold on the contemporary world. It empties meaning from the world, and she dies on the voyage back to England, having been excused from acting as witness at Aziz's trial for assaulting Adela. For Adela herself, the experience is inevitably profoundly disturbing, and it seems to prove the case of the British colonialists at the Club that all attempts, even of the most well-meaning and casual kind, to 'go native' are doomed. Most tellingly, perhaps, although Fielding is a lone voice defending Aziz's innocence, their friendship is shaken. This division is confirmed in the novel's final chapter, where the two are briefly reunited and a radicalized Aziz calls for the British withdrawal from India.

Intriguingly, Forster intimates towards the end of the book that the racial and religious incomprehension the incident at the Marabar dramatizes impacts directly upon established ideas of literary and artistic form. It falsely seems as if the outcome of the confusion there will resolve itself into another of the social comedies in which Forster had specialized earlier in his career. As one of several educated Indian voices in the book speculates, 'Cyril would marry Miss Quested – he grew certain of it ... It was the natural conclusion of the horrible senseless picnic' (p. 277). Yet, only a few pages afterwards, the narrative voice interrupts its own description of a concert of Hindu music in order to re-establish a division between differing racial understandings of genre. 'They did not one thing which the non-Hindu would feel dramatically correct; this approaching triumph of India was a muddle (as we call it), a frustration of reason and form' (p. 282). The inscriptions on banners hung around the concert venue confirm the cross-cultural textual confusion: 'God si Love. Is this the final message of India?'

Forster's method in the novel is significant in relation to other modernist texts which appropriate African or Sanskrit artefacts as examples of 'otherness' to offer further potentialities of reconciliation for a Western culture which is fragmented and uncertain in the wake of the First World War. *A Passage to India*, like Kipling's stories, enables the reader with insights into native culture and contradiction. The intellectual circle around Aziz, for example, is vividly and unidealistically drawn. Fielding is a strong character, respected by the local community for his knowledge and sympathy. Yet, at the end of the novel, Aziz's resistance to Fielding, on both personal and political levels, ensures the impossibility of formal or cross-cultural resolution (p. 316):

> 'if it's fifty or five hundred years we shall get rid of you, yes, we shall drive every blasted Englishman into the sea, and then' – he rode against him furiously – 'and then,' he concluded, half kissing him, 'you and I shall be friends.'

Forster's is a realistic narrative which concludes that, in this context of racial encounter, Western models of 'reason and form', including that of this kind of novel, are stressed almost to breaking point, and that they *must* be broken if new kinds of inter-racial cultural and literary possibility are to emerge. But this is a matter of history also. The despairing (because it is impossible in the time of the novel) but radical message at the end of the book is that it is only in the post-imperial situation that races can truly connect. The book does not seek to 'rationalize' its own uncertainties, such as by revealing what really did happen to Adela at the Marabar. But it dramatizes rather the liberal imperial guilt and deep uncertainties about the purpose and image of the empire after the European catastrophe of 1914–18. Forster began writing the book just before the war, and only completed it long after. Neither Western nor Eastern spiritual values offer any consolation here.

A similar sense of irresolution hangs over the short stories by the New Zealand writer Katherine Mansfield, who, from her colonial settler perspective, offered compelling and excoriating snapshots of modern culture and

London life, as well as more overtly autobiographical tales from her childhood. Occasionally in the writing, recalling scenes from her past, she strikes
a different note – one in which the sketched sociable surface of the text
opens to something else. In 'The Woman at the Store' (1911), for instance,
some drifters come to a sinister realization that the woman of the title, the
owner of a small local store where they stay, has murdered her husband. But
the eerie atmosphere of the story, the sense that something indefinable is
wrong, is mapped onto the landscape of the country itself:

> Down in the paddock I could hear Jo singing and the sound of the
> hammer strokes as Jim drove in the tent pegs. It was sunset. There is
> no twilight in our New Zealand days, but a curious half-hour when
> everything appears grotesque – it frightens – as though the savage
> spirit of the country walked abroad and sneered at what it saw.[16]

That 'savage spirit' is close to the quality which Mansfield's friend D. H.
Lawrence would later describe in Australia and Mexico in his novels of the
1920s. But it also casts a different kind of light upon Mansfield's own
satirical work about, say, modern relationships ('The Honeymoon',
'Marriage à la Mode', etc.), suggesting that, from her outsider's perspective,
she is particularly able to puncture the thin urban veneer. Further,
Mansfield's alertness to such alien qualities in her native country brings a
disturbing note to other of her stories describing colonial family life.
'Prelude', the longest and most complete of all her stories, was written in the
aftermath of the First World War. It narrates the move of a household of
several generations of women from the shore to an unspecified location
inland. For much of its length, the story is concerned with the dreams and
desires of the women in the house which are raised by the shift in scene. A
disturbing note is brought about by the presence near the new house of a
strange plant, however. The plant is particularly alluring to the most
sympathetic of the daughters, Kezia (p. 34):

> 'Mother, what is it?' asked Kezia.
>   Linda looked up at the fat swelling plant with its cruel leaves and
> fleshy stem. High above them, as though becalmed in the air, and yet
> holding fast to the earth it grew from, it might have had claws instead
> of roots. The curving leaves seemed to be hiding something; the blind
> stem cut into the air as if no wind could ever shake it.
>   'That is an aloe, Kezia,' said her mother.

The plant stands as a kind of symbol for the ambiguities of the women's
situation in this society, the hiddeness of lives and desires it is the story's
purpose to partly reveal. And yet it is something more than that, something

disgusting and doubtfully vegetable or animal, masculine and feminine, permanent and potentially dangerous. Later in the story, the aloe seems about to flower, which it is said to do only once in a hundred years. And yet this, and the possible suggestion of some kind of fulfilment within these lives at this spot, is left unclear. The mother admires, rather, 'the long sharp thorns that edged the aloe leaves, and at the sight of them her heart grew hard'. The aloe seems rather to stand for the toughness and threat of this new land, for the necessary qualities of survival and endurance which it demands, and to this extent mirrors the necessary qualities which women must obtain in order to endure their modern social and marital roles.

Once again, therefore, we find Mansfield discovering some of her most ambiguous but powerful symbolism in the fauna or climate of her native soil, a symbolism which re-focuses some of the undercurrents in her modern tales of women's constrained lives in the metropolis. Her outsider's perspective on this modern consciousness and constraint is underwritten by her early sense of the strangeness of her experience to modern literary expression. It is an experience which unsettles resolved forms and expectations, casting a different spiritual and tonal light on the writing and ensuring its disturbing modernist status.

The Greeks and the unconscious

In the wake of Frazer's study of the origins of primitive magic and ritual there arose a renewed interest in the interrelation between religion, culture, and civilization in the ancient Greek world. Jane Harrison, a classical scholar, Freudian, and pioneer for women's rights much admired by Virginia Woolf, wrote *Ancient Art and Ritual* in 1911, which connected all of these strains. Gilbert Murray's *Four Stages of Greek Religion* of 1912 carried the debate, in Frazer's fashion, back to more ancient sources. The early part of the twentieth century, therefore, saw renewed energy devoted to considering the beliefs, models, and patterns for understanding contemporary society and consciousness provided by the Greeks. Jacob, in Woolf's *Jacob's Room*, is preoccupied by the virtues of Greece and its civilization (he eventually travels there), and by the comparison between the ancient world and the modern, as becomes clear during a self-aggrandizing discussion Jacob has with a male friend (Greece is a male world in this book) (pp. 63–4):

> when all's said and done, when one's rinsed one's mouth with every literature in the world ... it's the flavour of Greek that remains ...

surveying all this, looming through the fog, the lamplight, the shades
of London, the two young men decided in favour of Greece.

'Probably,' said Jacob, 'we are the only people in the world who know
what the Greeks meant.'

The uniqueness of that moment in history, whereby the modern city streets
are seen to give way before the ancient civilization with a proclaimed understanding ('we know what the Greeks meant'), is due to a variety of factors.

Not the least of these was the fact that the 'ancient stories', relayed
through Homer and through the Greek tragic dramatists, had recently
acquired renewed currency for Woolf's and the modernists' generation.
Troy, the site of the *Iliad* and of the cataclysmic war over Helen, had for
thousands of years been presumed to be non-existent, a literary mythic
place. But its remains were discovered in 1870, by the archaeologist
Heinrich Schliemann, at Hissarlik. More immediately, Sir Arthur Evans's
excavations in Crete in 1900–6 had led him to discover the labyrinth
supposedly built by Dedalus at Knossos for King Minos. What these
discoveries reinstituted was a sense of the proximity of literature to actual
historical event and to actual place. The Homeric stories, which had seemed
for so many centuries to hover somewhere between myth and unreality,
were brought back over towards some identifiable sense of 'fact', or at least
to some grounding in historical actuality. Myth and history, during the years
in which modernism was beginning to emerge, seemed more closely related
than they had done across the Christian era.

When James Joyce gives the odd name Stephen Dedalus to his alter ego in
the twinned novels *A Portrait of the Artist as a Young Man* and *Ulysses*,
therefore, it is in full knowledge of these discoveries. The name combines
that of the first Christian martyr, Stephen (ironically so, since this modern
Stephen holds beliefs opposed to those of his forebear), with that of the
proven 'supreme artificer' of the ancient world, who supposedly built the
labyrinth housing the Minotaur on Crete. More particularly, we find Joyce's
fictional character embroiled in the *history*, the intellectual debates, and
contexts, as well as the actual events (such as the death of Parnell, or the
king's visit to Dublin), of his time. *Ulysses* is founded upon selected episodes
of Homer's *Odyssey* (the account of its hero's adventures on his return
journey to Greece after the Trojan War). It seeks, in its precise details about
the streets and movements of the population of Dublin on a single day, 16
June 1904, to provide a map of the place as accurate as that of Troy and
Knossos provided by the archaeologists.

Fiction and place, fiction and history, past and present are here brought
into a new kind of fruitful alliance, as T. S. Eliot recognized in his keynote

essay of admiration about Joyce's novel, '*Ulysses*, Order, and Myth' (1923). For Eliot, Joyce's 'mythical method' enables the novelist to give a shape to the 'futility and anarchy' of contemporary history. Although Joyce's 'Bloomsday' is in 1904, the novel dates (and places) itself on its final page in 'Trieste–Zurich–Paris, 1914–1921'. The places in which the book was written, the time in which it was written, establish it amongst the 'unreal' European cities of the First World War. Myth and history elide into each other. However, Stephen's famous recognition in *Ulysses*, after he has delivered a history lesson to schoolboys, that 'History ... is a nightmare from which I am trying to awake', brings the Homeric frame of the story into other, Irish national concerns. In order to be a truly modern artist, Stephen acknowledges that he must throw off the violent history of colonial rule, which has 'gorescarred' his country. *Ulysses*, with its continuous analogy between the founding texts of Western literature and this modern attempt to 'forge the conscience' of the Irish race, makes claims to the status of a founding text for his country in the modern world.

The Anglo-Irish poet W. B. Yeats, in seeking to make his own distinctively national literature in the 1880s and 1890s, had had frequent recourse to Homer's example as the original remembrancer of a locally set war-torn history. Yeats was also the establisher in modern poetry of a romantic, local, and spiritual mode, who envisaged a range of cultural possibilities he hoped the post-colonial Irish race would achieve. The Homeric in Yeats was often present in the complex symbolism of his love poems to Maud Gonne, who is represented as Helen of Troy, the most beautiful woman in the world, but also the cause of male tragedy and despair. But the Homeric also figured in much of Yeats's ambition to establish a separate Irish literature, which could stand in contradistinction to that of the colonizing force in his country, the British. In an essay of 1897, 'The Tribes of Danu', Yeats celebrated the significance of a local landscape as inspiration for the modern poet as for the ancient one. But he attached that celebration to a call for a return to the past in order to resist the prescribed literature from abroad:

> The poet is happy, as Homer was happy, who can see from his door mountains, where the heroes and beautiful women of old times were happy or unhappy, and quiet places not yet forsaken by the gods. I think that my own people, the people of a Celtic habit of thought ... can best begin [to recreate spiritual literature in the modern world], for they have a passion for their lands, and the waters and mountains of their lands remind them of old love tales, old battle tales.[17]

Joyce, with his sense of the necessity for modern literature, from whatever origin, to reflect the modern life of the city, would have been deeply sceptical of the tone and tenor of Yeatsian claims like this. Homer for Yeats is the founder of a national (and thence world) literature upon whom he can model himself and with whom he can align his own local, Celtic, and spiritual interests. Homer is, in his eyes, a romantic, not to say Romantic, figure of the courtly love tradition and celebrant of a close relationship with the local landscape (as Yeats was also of his childhood landscape in Sligo). Yet, despite what might seem alien qualities in such thinking by the older poet, Joyce has Stephen Dedalus remark upon the challenge that similar original and ancient perceptions of the relationship between humanity and the universe might offer to the writer seeking to achieve his own original work in this context. Nor is Joyce deaf to the nationalist implications of such a relationship in Ireland. Rather, Stephen Dedalus concludes, he must find some accommodation in his own thoughts and writing with such ancientness and primitiveness. The Greek 'mythical method' in *Ulysses* is, to an extent, then, a furthering of these cultural and nationalist debates within Ireland itself. There is a sense of Ireland as having a direct relationship to ancient literary sources which is independent (and politically so) from the use of those sources in mainstream literature from England.

For the American poet Ezra Pound, who edited Eliot's path-breaking sequence *The Waste Land* for him, the 'mythical method' also offered a practical solution to an ongoing problem of how to break away from perceived weaknesses in recent and contemporary verse. Greek literature had underpinned the retrospective impetus of Imagism, the 'movement' in poetry Pound had been engaged in promoting in the early 1910s. Its retrospective possibility had been concerned to cut away a perceived vagueness and concurrent sentimentality in English writing, and to open poetry in English to a wider rhythmic possibility than had been operative since the Renaissance. But Pound's reading of Imagist opportunity does not always acknowledge the full expressiveness and political edginess to which that possibility is being put.

In H. D.'s work, which Pound first puffed with the Frenchified term 'Imagiste', the Greek often stands in for a distillation of vocabulary and expression which counters the standard English iambic pentameter line and those sentimental expressions of lyricism familiar in Victorian poetry. In 'Hermes of the Ways', from H. D.'s wartime collection *Sea Garden* (1916), for example, the opening runs: 'The hard sand breaks, / and the grains of it / are clear as wine'. So far, so good, from the Poundian perspective. However, significantly what he is deaf to is the way that H. D.'s Greek primitivism, although running counter to contemporary lyric expectation, also mounts its own resistance to the masculinist aesthetics (such as Pound's own) and, of course, politics and militarism of the time:

The boughs of the trees
are twisted
by many bafflings . . .

But the shadow of them
is not the shadow of the mast head
nor of the torn sails.[18]

Hermes, as the messenger god of the Greeks, does not, in H. D.'s view (and this is in itself a message about poetry as much as it is about all language), offer clarity of communication. He is described in the poem as 'dubious', itself a doubled, punning word, meaning both sceptical about his own powers to convey his message properly and also not to be trusted as the bearer of truths. Contrary to Pound's Imagist propaganda about the sculptural hardness of the radically modern poem, therefore, H. D. sees in such 'clear as wine' lyricism simply further 'bafflings' and failures of translation. Further, she seems to imply that this paradoxically offers a potentiality in poetic imagery, *because of its very difficulty and complication*, which is not available in the contemporary world of war and the damage of 'torn sails'. For the woman poet, the Greek offers not only, therefore, a sifting away of detritus and the re-establishment of traditional poetic vision, it also offers a further complication, one that is resistant to easy translation and comprehension. For H. D., in other words, the (often classical) image or Image is subject to buffetings and uncertainties which challenge its lapidariness and transcendentalism from both within and without.

From his masculine perspective, Pound across the latter half of the 1910s was wrestling with similar questions about the relationship of the single image, however perfectly sculpted and defined, and the larger forces of erosion, decay, and history. From 1915 to 1917 he was working on longer poems which were eventually published in 1917 as 'Three Cantos'. But it is clear that he only moved towards understanding a way of orchestrating a longer poem (that 'rag-bag' which the first of these 1917 Cantos describes as a necessity for 'the modern world . . . to stuff all its thought in') through his reading of passages from Joyce's epic as they appeared in the *Little Review*. This process was concentrated, a bit later, through his work with Eliot's long sequence. His sense of Homer's *Odyssey* as providing a model for a narrative of journeying and episodic encounter led him to cut and paste a passage from the end of the original third of the 'Three Cantos' and set it at the start of his own epic voyage: 'And then went down to the ship, set keel to breakers, / Forth on the godly sea'.[19] When the passage reappeared at the opening of *Drafts and Fragments of XXX Cantos* in 1930, the lineation had changed and some of the archaisms had been eradicated. But Homer was again offering a way for the modern poet to pick a way through the 'futility' of the modern world.

The purpose of the passage these lines introduce has now been clarified. Through a complex interlayering of translation, Canto I re-renders the passage in Book 11 of Homer's *Odyssey* in which the hero Odysseus visits the blind prophet Tiresias in the underworld in order to understand his destiny. In order to summon the shades of the dead, Odysseus, or the poet voicing Odysseus' actions in this modern version by Pound, must 'pour libations' to the dead, and make bloody sacrifices. Pound's translation of one line here, 'dark blood flowed in the fosse', could, of course, relate to the contemporary experience in the battlefields of World War One. Like Woolf in *Jacob's Room*, his rendering of the male possibility of understanding through the Greeks is haunted by the mass deaths in his own time. But by so framing his epic by deploying the 'mythical method' in Joyce's fashion, Pound is presenting a version of history and modernity in which the past haunts (literally, through language and stories) and overwrites the present. It is also a version in which the present can only be understood by coming to a recognition of the ancient past. Pound's own 'method' in relaying this itself recognizes the difficulties ('bafflings') in establishing the message. In order to convey the 'primitiveness' of the Homeric encounter with the dead, Pound draws upon the rhythms and intonations he had learnt through his 1911–16 version of the Anglo-Saxon poem 'The Seafarer'. Canto I also reminds us that Homer has already been translated and retranslated across history as a new way of 'rebeginning' culture or civilization – not least in Renaissance versions of his epic and hymns in Latin. But the point beneath these complexities remains: that for Pound, as for H. D., Joyce, Woolf, and Yeats, the Greek had held an essence, a map of culture and spiritual possibility, which subsequent interlayerings and religions, including Christianity, had succeeded in obscuring and distorting. Each writer sees it as their *modern* purpose to recover, as archaeologists like Schliemann were recovering, the traces where possible of those original sources of enlightenment.

In making this return to the ancient originals in order to discover some understanding of contemporary cultural and aesthetic necessities, these writers reflected broader European thinking of the time. Most famously, perhaps, *The Birth of Tragedy* (1872) by the German philosopher Friedrich Nietzsche had sought, through its enquiry into the origins of dramatic form in Greece, to establish the relation between religion and art in the modern era. Nietzsche's understanding that tragedy arises out of the conflict between two religious possibilities – that presented by Apollo (god of order, light, and reason), and that of Dionysus (god of frenzy, wine, and unreason) – resonates behind similar tensions and dichotomies in the modernist period. His delineation of the tensions between control and its lack bears some similarities in its turn with the mapping of control and repression in Sigmund Freud's enquiries about the human consciousness, which had increasing popular currency at this time. Freud's sense that our daylight understanding is haunted and contradicted by repressed traumas and inarticulacies which require 'interpretation' by the analyst partakes of that 'primitive'/'civilized' splitting within modern consciousness envisaged by contemporary anthropology. But this is again infused by Freud's literary sensibility. His most famous popular notion, that of the 'Oedipus complex' (which he revisited and re-explained in *Totem and Taboo*) is, after all, indebted to Sophocles' tragic dramas.

The question of *direct* influence between these European reconsiderations of the ancient Greek world and Anglo-American modernism is various and sometimes more vague than literal. Pound, in an early poem, 'Redondillas, Or Something of That Sort', a poem wisely rejected from his 1911 collection *Canzoni*, mentions having read Nietzsche amongst others, and believing in 'some parts'. But, 'I prefer to read him in sections'.[20] Virginia Woolf, whose work on the consciousness, including the traumatized consciousness, had altered the purpose and shape of the modern novel, only began to systematically read Freud at the start of the *Second* World War. Her earlier understanding had largely been through popular hearsay and the discussions of Freud's work in her Bloomsbury coterie in the early 1920s, when the Woolfs' Hogarth Press began publication of a translation of Freud's complete works.

Whatever the exact contact with the work of thinkers like Nietzsche and Freud, however, what Anglo-American modernism shared with both was a preoccupation with what the latter in a book title of 1930 called *Civilisation and its Discontents*. In seeking both to provide models of the former term and to explain reasons for their feeling of the latter, all of these writers returned themselves to imaginary versions of the classical world of Greece, and set it in ironic and admonitory relationship to their various presents.

Notes

1 D. H. Lawrence, *Women in Love*, edited by Charles Ross (Harmondsworth, 1989), p. 133.
2 Sir James G. Frazer, *The Golden Bough: An Abridged Edition* (London, 1978), pp. 931–3.
3 In Britain, in the years preceding and during the First World War, there was a serious sign of decline in Christian practice, with the loss in some instances of over a third of the church-attending population across the period covered by this book. Increasing urbanization and social complexity, allied to competition from

recreational and other leisure outlets, meant that the visible status of the church in the state was further diminished beyond the already weaker profile from the last years of the nineteenth century. See John Stevenson, *British Society 1914–1945* (Harmondsworth, 1990), pp. 356ff.

4 *Blast 1*, edited by Wyndham Lewis (Santa Rosa, 1997), p. 33.

5 Joseph Conrad, *The Heart of Darkness*, edited by Robert Hampson (Harmondsworth, 1995), p. 18.

6 Virginia Woolf, *Mrs Dalloway*, edited by Claire Tomalin (Oxford, 1992), p. 34.

7 Virginia Woolf, *Jacob's Room*, edited by Sue Roe (Harmondsworth, 1992), p. 43.

8 See Samuel Hynes, *The Edwardian Turn of Mind* (Princeton, 1968), pp. 325–35.

9 D. H. Lawrence, *The Plumed Serpent* (Harmondsworth, 1981), pp. 402, 341.

10 *A Choice of Kipling's Verse*, edited by T. S. Eliot (London, 1963), p. 140.

11 Such concerns have been, from the point of view of the colonized peoples, instrumental in the development of theories about postcolonialism. Homi K. Bhabha's notion of 'hybridity', from his famous essay 'Signs Taken for Wonders' and other essays, for instance, sees language imposed upon colonized peoples as suffering subversive deformation and displacement, so that 'all sites of discrimination and domination' established by the language are undermined. See Bhabha's *The Location of Culture* (London, 1994), p. 114.

12 James Joyce, *A Portrait of the Artist as a Young Man*, edited by Seamus Deane (Harmondsworth, 1992), p. 204.

13 Such urgency had itself formed the currency of Irish nationalism from the 1890s, a nationalism with which Joyce was partly in disagreement as to the means, if not to the ends. A famous lecture by Douglas Hyde in 1892, 'On the Necessity for De-Anglicizing the Irish People', for instance, included a strong anti-materialist argument.

14 E. M. Forster, *A Room With a View*, edited by Oliver Stallybrass (Harmondsworth, 1990), p. 76.

15 E. M Forster, *A Passage to India*, edited by Oliver Stallybrass (Harmondsworth, 1987), p. 160.

16 Katherine Mansfield, *Collected Stories* (Harmondsworth, 1981), p. 554.

17 *Uncollected Prose by W. B. Yeats*, vol. II, edited by John P. Frayne and Colton Johnson (London, 1975), p. 55.

18 H. D., *Selected Poems* (Manchester, 1989), pp. 13, 15.

19 Ezra Pound, *Personae: The Shorter Poems*, edited by Lea Baechler and A. Walton Litz (New York, 1990), p. 243.

20 *Collected Early Poems of Ezra Pound*, edited by Michael John King (New York, 1976), p. 217.

|5|

Modernism, nationalism, and gender

The sense of distinctiveness shared by many modernist writers, which was described in Chapter 1, had its origin in national, cultural, and social uncertainties. These emerged in Ireland and America, as well as in Britain, at the turn of the nineteenth century into the early twentieth. For Britain, as I have argued, this was the time of vast national and imperial dominance. But it was also a time of increasing disturbance of the earlier order of things both internally and externally, and with both positive and negative results. Greater population mobility meant that many people were exposed for the first time to the growing metropolitan spaces. The election of a Liberal government in 1906, with its determined programme of welfare reform including pension rights and unemployment insurance, raised real hopes for the alleviation of poverty in the major industrial cities and beyond. The notion of state intervention in these matters finally brought an end to the Victorian era.

At the same time, the rise of socialist ideas from the 1880s onwards challenged the established delineation of the British class system. This, together with growing Liberal intervention in determining wage scales, along with rising prices at the time, meant that from 1910 onwards wave upon wave of industrial unrest ensued. There were strikes in the mines in 1910–11 and again in 1912, on the railways in 1911 and at seaports in 1910–11. For the first time, labour was withdrawn on a huge national scale for the purpose of broad political ends. The Liberal government found it even harder to contain the ongoing campaign to obtain votes for women. The party had been pledged to support the women's cause since 1902, and the 1906 election delivered a parliament broadly in favour of it. The rise of the suffrage movement after its re-emergence in the late 1890s altered for good the balance of relations in the home and the workplace. Yet, in government, the Liberals delayed implementing their pledge, and were therefore faced with growing militancy from women's groups right up to the First World War. Increasingly, also, the country was challenged by ideas, influences, and new artforms from the other imperial capitals of Europe, and from the out-reaches of the empire itself. The war, of course, brought about the greatest challenge to national traditions and continuities. It forced writers situated in London to reconsider the forms and values that had held good through literature from the Renaissance.

Similar tension, as this chapter will show, between a sense of national identity and shifting social relations, was felt also in America and in Ireland at the time. Ireland's relationship to British rule became increasingly fraught across this period, as was seen in the description at the end of Chapter 3. Here, I will consider more broadly the quest for nationhood in modern Irish writing, as it disturbs traditional literary forms and seeks to define a dis-tinctive conscience. America's sense of itself as an emergent culture too will be reviewed, as this established a key division in American authors' sense of the potential directions of modern literature. In the second part of the chapter, I will concentrate on the other central social issue in Britain and the United States across the period, the question of gender, which had revolu-tionary impact upon both the shape and the content of many of the major modernist texts.

Modernist nations

The period from 1880 to the outbreak of the First World War in 1914 saw the rise of a dramatically transformed and newly energized political ideal, nationalism. The arrival of democracy and universal education in America and across Europe brought a greater association between the individual and the nation state. Nations sought to achieve patriotism in their peoples, derived from a linguistically and administratively homogenized civil society. In America, for instance, knowledge of English was made a precondition of citizenship, and, from the late 1880s onwards, every school paid homage daily to the American flag. The significance of this separate national identity culminated in President Woodrow Wilson's 'Fourteen Points' about interna-tional diplomacy following the 1914–18 war – ideas which were crucial to the concluding treaty signed at Versailles. Wilson saw the future defined through a League of distinctive nations and sought bureaucratic mecha-nisms to obtain it. However, this visible display of national unity did not, as we shall see, serve to establish a settled definition of what this newly emergent American national consciousness might be. This further issue of identity preoccupied modernist writing from the US.

Moreover, from this time onwards, parts of the United Kingdom that had found themselves ruled by London for centuries began to define a sense of separate national identity with new vigour. In Ireland, from the 1890s onwards, this took the form of a cultural and language movement, which eventually led to the Easter 1916 uprising. In Scotland, such trends were concentrated in literature by the mid-1920s around the work of the communist poet Hugh MacDiarmid. In *Sangshaw* (1925) and his masterpiece, *The Drunk Man Looks at the Thistle* (1926), MacDiarmid deployed a synthetic version of the Scots language, which he called 'Lallans', to meditate upon the identity of his nation and its historical sufferings. Modernist writing displays, therefore, a shifting relationship to nationhood, but one in which it is constantly seeking a defining role for itself with regard to its national context.

The disturbing concatenation of circumstances described above often forced English writers back upon themselves, into reviewing the nature of their national tradition. D. H. Lawrence, for instance, published a collection of short stories in 1922 called *England, My England*, in the title story of which a disaffected and lost father seriously hurts his daughter by negligence, leaves home, and dies in the trenches. It is as though Lawrence feels that the whole national tradition of pastoral literature has been irredeemably finished (the work opens, like many of Lawrence's, with a prose hymn to the English countryside). But those writers from America and Ireland who form pivotal figures in the period were in a wholly different situation from the English one as regards their ideas about the relationship of their work to writing from the past. For instance, in a lecture which he gave in Dublin in 1936, on 'Tradition and the Practice of Poetry', T. S. Eliot reviewed his debt to the British poets of the 1890s. He said that 'I certainly had much more in common with them than with the English poets who survived to my own day – there were no American poets at all.'[1] This sweeping aside seems to assert that there had never been an American precursor to whom Eliot could look for his own writing. There is no single essay in the prose work he himself collected during his lifetime relating wholly to an American figure. Eliot's revolutionary writing, therefore, is consciously created, as Henry James's had been, from the encounter between his own sensibility and that cultural tradition which he recovered from Europe.

Eliot's erstwhile mentor and editor, Ezra Pound, showed a similar resistance to influence from within his native tradition, even though he also was often preoccupied by it. It was not until the poems of 1913–15 gathered in *Lustra* that he famously declared 'A Pact' between himself and Walt Whitman, the major American poet of the nineteenth century. But, in doing so, he manifested continuing ambiguity and strain in the relationship.

Whitman is the 'pig-headed' father to Pound's child, and Whitman is cast in the poem as something of an unsophisticated pioneer into new territory: 'It was you that broke the new wood, / Now is the time for carving.'[2] In a slightly earlier poem addressed to New York, 'N.Y.', Pound had shown a similarly awkward relation to his national inheritance in a hymn to one of America's metropolitan and artistic centres. In this self-dialogue, the poem's speaker instructs the city, figured as a young girl, to 'Listen! Listen to me, and I will breathe into thee a soul' (once again the gendering of Pound's poetic practice is to the fore here, as in his treatment of women poets such as H. D.). Yet the opposing voice in the poem argues that the poet has no power to create such animating music. Besides, this voice acknowledges that the conceit of the poem is false in the modern age where the city is filled with traffic rather than being maid-like. Yet the final verse reasserts the opening injunction, 'Listen to me!' and the sense that it is for the poet to create meaning, or 'a soul', for a place that is otherwise cast as empty of significance (p. 58).

'N.Y' is an early work which shows Pound's pre-Raphaelite musicality at war with his resolutely modern sensibility. It is interesting, since this war was fought rarely for him in subjects relating to his native soil. The call 'Listen to me!' reveals Pound's doubts about his ability to speak to or for his American audience, whilst also seeking to woo it. In the long essay 'Henry James' of 1918, Pound reveals a similar scepticism when considering the achievement of the American, who for him, as for Eliot, formed the greatest example of a writer needing to establish a modern consciousness through engagement with the European past. Taking issue with a remark in the London *Times* suggesting that Americans would understand James's complex national identity, Pound sneers that 'The "Americans" will understand nothing whatsoever about it. They have understood nothing about it. They do not even know what they lost.' Only someone who has 'lived on both sides of the Atlantic', Pound avers, has any right to 'appraise Henry James'.[3] Even when writing of his friend and fellow poet William Carlos Williams, who, he admits, 'has been determined to stand or sit as an American', Pound seeks to unsettle Williams from his stance. He emphasizes Williams's view of America as that of the recent immigrant: 'he starts where an European would start if an European were about to write of America: sic: America is a subject of interest' (p. 392).

Whatever the worth of his assessment of Williams, we can see that the mobility and fluidity of Pound's modernist poetics, as well as Eliot's, was derived from a sense of the as yet unformed distinctiveness of 'America' or of its native poetry. Eliot was, of course, in 1927 to follow James's earlier example by taking full British citizenship. Pound on the other hand sought, as we shall see, increasingly troubling versions of an idealized national possibility in Fascist European leaders. However, this acknowledgement of the unformed nature of American potential, and thence of its imagination and art, was shared even by those writers who, like Williams, determined to establish a modern consciousness whilst remaining in America itself. In his essay 'The Noble Rider and the Sound of Words', the poet Wallace Stevens contemplated an undistinguished statue in Washington of the former president, Andrew Jackson. If the statue had been created by the Italian Renaissance sculptor Verrocchio, Stevens muses, 'the whole American outlook today might be imperial'. But, 'treating this work as typical, it is obvious that the American will as a principle of the mind's being is easily satisfied'. For Stevens, the statue, like the national 'will' or consciousness, is 'unreal' in every sense, and unrealized, the implication being, as with those modernists who sought 'reality' in Europe, that it is for the modern artists to bring reality, including national reality, closer.[4] Stevens's ideas about the perfectibility of the artistic imagination are aligned with the refinement of his nation's consciousness. In Williams's own innovative mixture of prose and poetry of 1923, *Spring and All*, there is a similar sense of vulnerability. The opening poem casts the American landscape as a pastoral wasteland, 'the / waste of broad, muddy fields', through which 'sluggish / dazed spring approaches':

> They enter the new world naked,
> cold, uncertain of all
> save that they enter.[5]

America is punningly envisioned as the life that appears after a long period of historical and cultural stasis, but uncertainty predominates over the sense of national purpose. The second part of the poem confirms that this somewhere is only beginning to awaken. It is a place of newly mixed profusion and blending, of 'Pink confused with white / flowers and flowers reversed', but the new beauty is rudimentary and unresolved or refined.

The ambiguities felt here, and by Pound's speaker in the poem 'N.Y.', find their echo several years later in the situation of the protagonist of the Irishman James Joyce's novel *A Portrait of the Artist as a Young Man* (1916). Shared by all of these works is an assertion of the artist's duty to use his ability to breathe life into an emergent nation. Joyce's hero, Stephen Dedalus, during his time as a student at University College Dublin, is subjected to several versions of Irish nationalist idealism in his encounters with his fellow students. Ireland was at this time still under British rule. From the 1890s onwards, however, what Roy Foster calls 'The "New" Nationalism' had been aroused, accompanied by the latest in a series of land reforms allowing agricultural workers to purchase the land they worked. There was renewed agitation amongst labour organizations, and an air of cultural revivalism, which created an unprecedented period of strife in the north and south of the island from 1912 to 1922.[6]

It is in Dedalus's disagreements with his 'peasant student' friend Davin that his attitude to contemporary versions of Irish nationalism, and his counter-formulation of the true nature of the country, become clear. Davin is a supporter of the Gaelic Athletic Association (established in 1884) and of the Gaelic League (which flourished in the 1890s and early into the new century). Both movements urged the de-Anglicization of Ireland through the revival of an 'original' version of its national sports and culture; the Gaelic League sought the revival of the Irish language as the national tongue, and brought about a renewal literature written in Gaelic. Dedalus is adamant in his resistance to Davin's urging that his nationality and his Catholicism mean that he must join the cause ('In your heart you are an Irishman but your pride is too powerful'). Instead, he takes a fatalistic, if realistic, view of the results of his country's colonization by the British:

> My ancestors threw off their language and took another, Stephen said. They allowed a handful of foreigners to subject them. Do you fancy I am going to pay in my own life and person debts they made?[7]

Stephen's refusal is to bow before the seeming demands of his religion, nationalism, and the presumed linguistic imperatives of his country's historical situation. 'I shall try to fly by those nets', he famously says. For him, the attitude of such as Davin is two steps backwards from a contemporary acceptance of the reality of Ireland's historical plight. To adopt Gaelic is to be blind to the fact that English is irrevocably the language of the country, however the language is inflected in Ireland through local dialects (as shown through Dedalus's encounter with his English Dean of Studies). Attitudes such as Davin's enforce upon Stephen the sense that Ireland is a self-devouring country, unable to achieve a modern and independent sense of its own identity. By the end of the book, he accepts that it is the artist's duty to create: 'I go to encounter for the millionth time the reality of experience and to forge in the smithy of my soul the uncreated conscience of my race' (pp. 275–6). 'Forge' is finely balanced as a term. Like Pound, Williams, and Stevens from the American perspective, Dedalus acknowledges that 'conscience' is as much a matter of the literary imagination as it is one of political efficacy. The modern artist can rely upon no earlier models in the native literary tradition adequate to the contemporary national blight.

Joyce's next novel, *Ulysses* (1922), no less than the polyglot babble of his last work *Finnegan's Wake* (1939), establishes that the modern conscience is subject to a complex of influences which continue to resist what he sees as the available monocular vision of many versions of Irish nationalism. Faced by the hostile questioning of a group of nationalist supporters, the Jewish Leopold Bloom, the hero of *Ulysses*, stands his ground:

> – What is your nation if I may ask, says the citizen.
> – Ireland, says Bloom. I was born here. Ireland.
> The citizen said nothing only cleared the spit out of his gullet.[8]

In a lecture he gave in 1907, 'Ireland: Island of Saints and Sages', Joyce had fully acknowledged the appalling history visited upon his country by the colonizing British. 'Does the slave's back forget the rod?', he inquired, and blamed the current backwardness and poverty of the country upon 'English laws' and 'the negligence of the English government'. But, at the same time, he asks:

> What race or language . . . can nowadays claim to be pure? No race has less right to make such a boast than the one presently inhabiting Ireland. Nationality . . . must find its basic reason for being in something that surpasses . . . changeable entities such as blood or human speech.[9]

His assertion of this fact did not change across his subsequent writing life. His nationalism is both open-ended and self-aware.

Questioning the nature of singular versions of national identity in this way, Joyce is furthering earlier issues concerning the relation of literary to national identity from within his different inheritance by the Anglo-Irish poet W. B. Yeats. Yeats's attempts to resolve tensions and contradictions between, on the one hand, the historical realities of his country, and, on the other, the version of it in his ideal imagining, is wholly different. Musing in his diary towards the end of *A Portrait of the Artist as a Young Man* upon Michael Robartes, an alter ego adopted by Yeats in various of his poems and prose works, Stephen Dedalus concludes (p. 273) that Robartes

> remembers forgotten beauty and, when his arms wrap her around, he presses in his arms the loveliness which has long faded from the world. Not this. Not at all. I desire to press in my arms the loveliness which has not yet come into the world.

Joyce's aesthetic sensibility is, therefore, resolutely forward-looking, towards shaping a reality which has not yet been achieved. For Yeats, in contrast, modernity presents a much more troubling and potentially disruptive picture. *His* version of Ireland, from the time of the early 1890s in works like 'To the Rose upon the Rood of Time' (discussed in Chapter 1), had been deeply imbued by his mystical and aesthetic beliefs. Writing in tune with a Romantic tradition that includes William Blake and Percy Bysshe Shelley, Yeats emphasized, much as Stephen Dedalus was later to do, the importance of the individuality of the artist in founding the undefined national sensibility. As Yeats noted in 1908,

> All literature in every country is derived from models, and as often as not these are foreign models, and it is the presence of a personal element alone that can give it nationality in a fine sense, the nationality of its maker.[10]

For Yeats as for Joyce, nationality cannot be extricated from the creative process. But, at this stage and later in his career, Yeats's version of that nationality cannot be construed outside personality, or the personalities of a few chosen individuals. In the grand lament of 'September 1913', included in *Responsibilities* (1914), Yeats juxtaposes what he sees as the degenerate capitalism of the burgeoning class of small Catholic shopkeepers in modern Ireland with the heroic tradition of nationalism which had existed in the country from the 1690s. 'Romantic Ireland's dead and gone, / It's with O'Leary in the grave.'[11] John O'Leary, a nationalist and Fenian who served as Yeats's mentor as a young man in Dublin, had died in 1907. With that passing, and with the earlier passing in 1891 of Charles Stewart Parnell (a passing much lamented in Joyce also[12]), Yeats felt that the possibility of a distinctive national identity emerging through politics had disappeared.

Yeats was, however, increasingly marginalized by the actual movements towards Irish independence which gained pace after the rebellion in 1916. He experienced at first hand the feuding between various groups in the civil war of 1922–3, in the wake of the Anglo-Irish Treaty signed late in 1921. Later, as a senator in the new Free State, he witnessed what he felt to be the neglect of the ideals of his Protestant forebears. Yeats's later works seek, therefore, to celebrate an alternative Irish tradition to that national political view which held sway for the last seventeen years of his life. Later poems like 'Coole Park, 1929', 'Coole and Ballylee, 1931', 'Blood and the Moon', and 'The Municipal Gallery Re-Visited', are all nostalgic. But they are nostalgic now for the Anglo-Irish tradition of which he had himself been a direct beneficiary through the patronage of the owner of the Georgian house at Coole Park, Lady Gregory.

This was a tradition centred upon the society of the so-called Big Houses of Ireland, houses often owned by former colonial administrators, where it was possible to 'meditate' away from the modern bustle of the city. 'Coole Park, 1929' reflects on the creative power of such places: 'Thoughts long knitted into a single thought, / A dance-like glory that those walls begot'

(p. 243). It is in such places, as 'Blood and the Moon' symbolically asserts, that the most prominent writers and thinkers of eighteenth-century Ireland, Oliver Goldsmith, Jonathan Swift, Edmund Burke, and Bishop Berkeley, had all flourished, and helped define the Anglo-Irish sensibility. In these latter years, therefore, Yeats's version of his personal and national identity is self-consciously crafted as a form of resistance to available national models. Unlike Joyce's version of that identity, which sought to establish a cosmopolitan openness, and which resists prejudice whilst recognizing cultural difference ('I was born here'), Yeats's Ireland of the mind from the early 1920s was very much one inflected by his hybrid inheritance. He was deeply fearful of the 'darkening flood' both of modernity and of Catholic nationalism.

What Joyce and Yeats shared with the Americans like Pound, Eliot, and Stevens, however, is a conflicted sense of uncertainty. They share anxiety and potential aesthetic freedom in the fact that no settled nationhood or national literary tradition was bequeathed to them from the past. Like Pound and Eliot, Joyce and Yeats are inherently restless writers. Yeats shuttled back and forth between the twin poles of his consciousness in London and Ireland. Joyce, assured early on of the need to 'fly by' the potentially entrapping nets of his national culture, moved repeatedly around mainland Europe in order paradoxically to forge his nation's conscience.

When these modernist writers did settle, as Eliot did in the wake of his 1927 taking of British citizenship, it was with a strong sense of the need to rediscover a version of stability within a national consciousness. Eliot's *Four Quartets*, the final three of which were written at the time of the Second World War, find him tuning into earlier moments in English history in order to re-establish purpose and vision which the war was threatening to disrupt. Eliot's sense of time and temporality in wartime echoes that so often registered by writers during the First World War. He sees war as a between-time in which various qualities have become intermixed. As the last-to-be-published Quartet, *Little Gidding* (1942), opens, 'Midwinter spring is its own season / Sempiternal though sodden towards sundown, / Suspended in time, between pole and tropic'. Yet it is this historical suspension, captured in the English countryside, which provides the opportunity for the kinds of harmonization and synthesis through history Eliot achieves in the final movement of his poem. (Little Gidding is a religious community in which King Charles I took shelter during his flight from his enemies at the time of the English Civil War.)

At this time of renewed conflict, Eliot establishes a sense of the means through which history, which might otherwise be figured as chaotic and futile, discovers an order and a pattern through the consonance of its 'timeless moments'. These are moments that can be read backwards and forwards through time: 'So, while the light fails / On a winter's afternoon, in a secluded chapel / History is now and England.'[13] This is a supremely patriotic statement at a time of national emergency, a resolution of the purgatorial uncertainties of Eliot's earlier *The Waste Land* as a new understanding of the relation of the local to wider religious and historical preoccupations. Eliot's synthetic conservatism in these matters, his version of English patriotism, is, however, relatively compelling when set alongside his compatriot Ezra Pound's shameful attempt to invent a version of nationhood through his admiration for the Italian Fascist dictator Benito Mussolini. Pound's 1935 *Jefferson and/or Mussolini* displayed a mistaken sense that it is for the artist to forge the true identity of a nation. In comparing one of the founders of independent America with Mussolini, Pound consistently returned to his sense of them as builders, constructors, practical men. Mussolini, like Jefferson, is an artist, and therefore someone only an artist such as Pound can truly understand. The desperation and unlikeliness of the comparison confirms the broader point made in this section of the chapter. Modernist writing is both driven by, and disturbed by, the urge to define and again define an unconfirmed sense of national culture and destiny. The modern phenomenon, nationalism, which has done so much to reshape and perturb the world, acted as a reshaping force also upon literary and formal consciousness in the first twenty years of the last century.

Modernism and gender

The re-emergence of the women's movement on both sides of the Atlantic from the late 1890s onwards had brought renewed impetus to the explorations of the position of women in society. This had been reflected in explorations of women's social situations and sexuality in the so-called New Women novels of the early part of the decade. In America, the reform movement to give women the vote gained its first breakthrough in the West in 1910–14, when women suffragists won the battle in nine states. The campaign grew across the 1910s, and votes for women were eventually entered into the Constitution of the whole country in 1920. In 1897 in Britain, the Union of Women's Suffrage Societies drew together groups calling for the vote which had been split since a decade earlier. In 1903, Emmeline Pankhurst and her daughters Christabel and Sylvia founded the Women's Social and Political Union, which originally had an interest in the plight of women more generally, beyond the pressing issue of the vote. This was reflected in the fact that the Union initially attracted high numbers of working-class women.

Extract 4 on pp. 143–4 comes from Emmeline Pankhurst's famous speech on 'The Importance of the Vote', from March 1908. Pankhurst spells out in exemplary terms the symbolic importance of the franchise, particularly at a time when the Liberal government in Britain was using social legislation in order actively to intervene in domestic life for the supposed good of the people. In response to the typical fear at the time of increasing racial degeneration, particularly amongst the working classes, a fear which we have encountered before in the run-up to the War and through it, the Liberals were proposing to ensure that mothers stayed in the home. Pankhurst's angry response that women are debarred from participating in the debate through their lack of the vote clearly establishes the tone of the argument about rights and empowerment for women which runs through British and American texts of the period by both male and female writers.

Across the decade, the British suffrage campaign became increasingly militant under the Pankhurst family's stewardship. In 1905 Christabel Pankhurst sought to disrupt an election meeting, an incident widely reported and disapproved of. With the failure of the Liberal government to honour its promises on the vote once in office, the movement started more immediate and often symbolic action against the markers of institutional power and finance. In 1909 the Union started a campaign of causing criminal damage, including breaking the windows of government buildings. When the women refused to pay the fines incurred, they were taken to prison. Sometimes they went on hunger-strike, risking starvation for the cause, bringing attempts to force-feed them from the prison authorities. There was a lull in the suffrage campaign in 1910–12, when it seemed that parliament was about to change its mind about the vote. But when the various Bills to give women the vote were defeated, the Union started a programme of destruction of the mail and an arson campaign in 1913. The suffrage campaign was aided by a series of plays and novels, including Elizabeth Robins's play *Votes for Women!* (1907) and Gertrude Colmore's *Suffragette Sally* (1911).

These plays, like many such works, blurred the boundaries between factual reportage and fiction, whilst also conferring the status of martyr upon those who suffered for the cause. In Colmore's play, for instance, the force-feeding of a suffragette is scandalously compared to the suffering undergone by Christ at the crucifixion. Nineteen-thirteen saw an act of real sacrifice in the heroic protest of Emily Wilding Davidson, who threw herself in front of the king's racehorse in that year's Derby. The First World War threw the campaign into abeyance. But 1918 brought a limited vote to those women over thirty who were local government electors, or who were married to local government electors (the Reform Bill of that year also extended male franchise to those over twenty-one, or to those over nineteen who had fought at the Front).

Male writers in England at this time and later responded to the suffragette movement with a reactionary mixture of anxiety and a need ultimately to present a repressive version of the status quo. In H. G. Wells's *Ann Veronica* (1909) the heroine strives to escape from her constricting suburban life, dominated by a father who fails to understand her entirely. When she escapes to London, seeking to continue her education as a biologist, Ann pursues her association with the suffragettes. She spends time in prison, having taken part in one of their acts of civil disobedience, an attempt to interrupt the proceedings of parliament. When 'Ann Veronica Puts Things in Order', to quote the title of the chapter narrating her release, however, her interests rapidly veer away from the cause, and the novel's centre of gravity shifts radically. Ann falls in love with the married technician at her laboratory, Capes, and the novel follows a romance plot through to the pair's elopement abroad. Wells's complacent conclusion about the cause of women's suffrage would seem to be that it does not answer to women's true need for freedom and recognition, which can only be discovered through a more equitable relationship between the sexes, even one that flouts convention. The true path of love must be obtained in spite of difficulties and in defiance of social and legal boundaries, as in this love between the young girl and the married man. Women's freedom is to live according to their emotional and sexual desires.

Wells's conclusion anticipates the prejudice against women's political aspirations expressed by later male writers, including D. H. Lawrence. Lawrence's 'Study of Thomas Hardy', on which he worked at the outbreak of the First World War in 1914, acknowledges that the suffragettes are 'certainly the bravest, and, in the old sense, most heroic party amongst us'. But he despairs that the movement is limited to the achievement of an equitable say in the workings of the state ('The women . . . want the vote in order to make more laws. That is the most lamentable and pathetic fact'). For Lawrence, this ambition confirms the 'sickness' into which life as a whole has descended. The machinery of state, in his view, is abusive of the true centres of life which 'lie in the heart' of man and woman. It prevents the founding of a new and true relationship between them: 'No wonder there is a war.' 'There is no need to break laws', he later concludes. 'The only need is to be a law unto oneself.' And to unite in relation with the opposite sex, in Lawrence's half-scientific, half-mystical version, 'the dual stream of woman and man, as the two waves meet and burst into foam, bursting into the unknown'. Lawrence's view of women in this essay's alternative, anti-political version of freedom, is deeply retrograde, and sometimes falls into rehearsing damaging clichés – 'Every man seeks in woman for that which is stable, eternal.'[14] His and Wells's dread at the prospect of women's political empowerment and women's rights is matched elsewhere in modernist writing by men, such as in Pound's masculine aesthetic discussed in the last chapter. It marks a real blindness that overshadows modernist aesthetics.

This is not to say that all modernist women's writing is necessarily at one with the tactics deployed by the suffragettes in order to obtain their rights. In Virginia Woolf's second novel, *Night and Day*, written during the war but published in 1919, there is scathing satire at the expense of the suffragettes. Mary Datchet, one of the novel's two heroines, works in an office of one of the suffrage movements. Woolf's picture of the movement through this lens is one of honest do-gooding of a deeply amateurish sort. But this dislike of the practical necessities of the campaign early in her writing career went along with a consistent preoccupation with the situation of women, their historical repression, and the conditions necessary for their freedom. This political drive to her concerns was closely aligned with her consistent concern with what it took for a woman in this hostile world to succeed as a writer.

By the time of her polemical essay *A Room of One's Own* (1929), Woolf settles upon the necessity of 'money and a room of her own' if a woman is to write fiction. The 'liberties and licences of a novelist' which she deploys in making her argument for a new kind of women's writing are inter-changeable in the essay with an awareness of a necessary correlative economic (£500 a year, she reckons) and spatial freedom for women in the modern city. Woolf casts her meditation upon these issues as taking place during a walk through London (much like Mrs Dalloway's walks at the opening of her novel). The development of her argument is performed and instigated by her awareness of the streets and monuments she passes: 'Walk through the Admiralty Arch (I had reached that monument) . . . and reflect upon the kind of glory celebrated there.'

What the public spaces and face of the city confirm is 'the patriarch's' 'instinct for possession, the rage for acquisition' which have impelled men to imperial adventure and to death on the battlefields of the First World War. Woolf's sudden acquisition of financial independence, through the £2,500 willed to her by an aunt in 1909, had, she recalls in this essay, opened totally new spaces for her, and freed her from the impositions of a male system of values and literary tradition:

> Indeed my aunt's legacy unveiled the sky to me, and substituted for the large and imposing figure of a gentleman, which Milton recommended for my perpetual adoration, a view of the open sky.[15]

The legacy, in other words, removed the obscuring presence of Christianity, and led to Woolf's questioning of all male rhetorical strategies and literary achievements. *A Room of One's Own* speculates instead upon the alternative rhythms and forms of a female tradition, 'for we think back through our mothers if we are women'. Woolf's writing seeks here and across her fiction from *Jacob's Room* onward to perform a new consciousness, one which resists the shape and structure of 'a man's sentence'. 'The book has somehow to be adapted to the body, and at a venture one would say that women's books should be shorter, more concentrated, than those of men' (pp. 69–70). Woolf, however, recognizes the transitional and improvisational nature of her essay. It is after all written at a historical moment in which many of these issues remained to be defined in a world still coming to terms with the 'shock' of the First World War and with women's different status in society (p. 13).

Despite her sense that the nature of writing across gender must correlate with the physical nature of the author, Woolf speculates in her essay, 'amateurishly', as she admits, on the essential androgyny of writing, and of humanity in its best moments. Looking down from her writing room upon a young couple getting into a taxi in the street below, she acknowledges 'a profound, if irrational, instinct in favour of the theory that the union of man and woman makes for . . . the most complete happiness'. She then muses on the possibility that each individual contains both male and female elements, with either one predominant according to the gender of the individual (pp. 88–9). This sense of the androgyny of the individual is something which Woolf playfully writes out in her trans-historical novel *Orlando* (1928), where the central figure of the book changes from being male to female halfway through. In despite of this idealized platonic model, however, the emphasis of *A Room of One's Own* is upon the duty of the woman novelist to re-explore the spaces of the city in order to understand the different nature of women's experience and lives lived there: 'All these infinitely obscure lives remain to be recorded, I said . . . and went on in thought through the streets of London feeling in imagination the pressure of dumbness, the accumulation of unrecorded life' (p. 81).[16]

Woolf's sense of the 'accumulation' of such lives, which is registered in the accumulation of her own clauses, and in the shape of her sentences, is shared with the most radical experimenter with sentence shapes in this period, the American lesbian writer Gertrude Stein. In her 1926 essay 'Composition as Explanation', an essay which Woolf published in England through her Hogarth Press, Stein both argues for, and exemplifies, in her writing, a necessary 'continuous present' in the process of composition:

The only thing that is different from one time to another is what is seen and what is seen depends on how everybody is doing everything. This makes the thing we are looking at very different and this makes what those describe it make of it, it makes a composition, it confuses, it shows, it is, it looks, it likes it as it is, and this makes what is seen as it is seen.[17]

How we are in the world at any one moment determines how we perceive the world, which in its turn determines how the literary composition is structured. For Stein (as for other modernists like the Eliot of *The Waste Land*), this means that modern writing is inevitably present-tense writing. As for Woolf, there is an intersection between the style of the composition and physical space, an accumulation of details which opens and expands the sentence. For Stein (though less obviously for Woolf, perhaps, despite her constant ambivalent attention to London as imperial capital), this is also a national trait. Stein makes this clear in the essay 'Poetry and Grammar', in which she meditates upon her epic novel of national foundation, *The Making of Americans*, which had eventually appeared in 1925 (p. 132):

> in achieving something that had neither the balance of a sentence nor the balance of a paragraph but a balance a new balance that had to do with a sense of movement of time included in a given space ... is a definitely American thing.
>
> An American can fill up space in having his movement of time by adding unexpectedly anything.

Stein's repetitions and variations push the temporal movement of the sentence as we read into a paradoxically more static and spatial dimension. Woolf's exploration in thought and writing of 'the streets of London' is similar in its ambition, yet, as we have seen, more explicitly gendered in its impulse.

Woolf's preoccupation with the gendering of space in the city, and its consequences for literary form and style, is consonant with reconsiderations made by women writers from both Britain and America across the period studied by this book. Towards the earlier part of that period, the American Edith Wharton had been conscious of the tragic consequences that might ensue when a woman innocently steps beyond convention and enters a male space. In *The House of Mirth* (1905), her heroine, Lily Bart, lives precariously upon society through the invitations she receives to stay with various wealthy women. But tragically one day she gives way on a whim to a request that she visit the rooms of the bachelor Lawrence Selden when she is in New York. She is seen leaving Selden's building by a wealthy businessman, Simon

Rosedale, and immediately understands the difficulties which are likely to ensue:

> Why must a girl pay so dearly for the least escape from routine? Why could one never do a natural thing without having to screen it behind a structure of artifice? She had yielded to a passing impulse in going to Lawrence Selden's rooms, and it was so seldom that she could allow herself the luxury of an impulse! This one, at any rate, was going to cost her rather more than she could afford.[18]

Indeed, it is going to cost her her life, as the novel traces Lily's fall, through her failure to marry and her increasing social isolation into poverty, despair, and an early death.

Later in this period, however, we find a new range of cultural and technological media deployed in arguments about the situation of women and questions about their situation. Virginia Woolf was an assiduous collector of newspaper clippings, and in *A Room of One's Own* makes a purportedly casual scanning of the daily newspaper over lunch the basis for an attack on the patriarchal nature of the English establishment. Other writers of the time, too, were viewing contemporary media as creating possibilities for women to establish their own spaces in the city. By the outbreak of World War One, Britain had over 3,000 cinemas. Films about the war played an important part in the recruitment drives, and the Cinema Division of the Department of Information put out documentaries relating to the war's major battles very soon after those battles had concluded. The film relating to the Battle of the Somme, which had begun on 1 July 1916, was released, for instance, on 21 August of that year. It was soon showing in over a thousand theatres, and played a major part in changing civilian attitudes to the war. Conspicuous by their absence in these films, of course, were the thousands of corpses of the slain.[19]

In the later 1920s, cinema was seen by some women writers as offering different kinds of possibility. In the important international magazine about film, *Close Up*, which ran from 1927 to 1933, the English novelist Dorothy Richardson published a series of articles in which she considered the impact of cinema upon a 'new audience'. This was an audience of women, who watched films during the day when their husbands were at work. Richardson notes the transformational effect upon 'tired women, their faces sheened with toil' wrought by the immediacy of the medium, its establishment of an 'inner relationship . . . intimate as thought' with its audience. She sees the presence of women *in* the movies as inherently liberating, bringing a new realism to the representation of women in art and releasing the 'full power' of those women watching the screen. 'Free from man's pitiful illusion of history, she sees everything in terms of life that uncannily she knows to be at all times fundamentally the same.'[20]

What is striking in Richardson's articles about the liberatory space of the cinema for women (as well as in the articles contributed to the magazine by one of its co-editors, the American poet H. D.) is that the *location* of the cinema in the city is crucial to the experience of the film. She will describe the situation and interior of the movie-house as part of the meaning of the film itself. For H. D., this description confirms the international possibilities opened by the relatively new medium ('Languages filter into my consciousness. French? German?'). For Richardson, however, the location of the cinema provides the establishment of an important female space within the dynamics of an expanding metropolis and of the British class structure. She is a supporter of local suburban cinema, and is against travelling to metropolitan centres to view movies ('we shall find our own place our best testing-ground . . . the small cinema that will remain reasonably in tune with the common feelings of common humanity'). In another piece, 'Cinema in Slum-Land', Richardson sees the liberating possibility of the medium for working-class women, by 'bringing cramped lives into communication with the general life . . . insensibly they are living new lives' (pp. 124, 169, 180).

Crucial to these women's sense of the immediate and universal communicative power of the movies, however, was the fact that it is silent cinema that they are discussing. Contributors to *Close Up* generally criticized the advent of the talkies, but Richardson is unique in seeing the transition in gendered terms. In a 1932 article, 'The Film Gone Male', Richardson recycled some stereotyped images of gender difference to powerful new effect. Women 'excel in memory' over men, Richardson claims; they are 'humanity's silent half'. With the arrival of the talkies, film is therefore fulfilling a masculine destiny, one that violates the 'universal, unchanging, unevolving verities' which are contained in memory. Cinema, in 'going male', enters a fallen state, 'the destiny of planful becoming rather than of purposeful being' (p. 205). The space for immediate imaginative and freeing connection between (female) audience and film surface, in specific locations and at particular moments of the day, is eroded by the directive inclusion of dialogue.

Implicit in Richardson's resistance to sound movies, as in that of other contributors to *Close Up*, is the resistance to the Americanization of the medium through Hollywood. These writers favour British and European film, and are dismissive of the perceived sentimentality of the increasingly dominant American import. It is a dismissal which is repeated elsewhere in writing by women at the time. The ironic male speaker of the New Zealand short-story writer Katherine Mansfield's 'Je Ne Parle Pas Français' asks herself:

> Why am I so bitter against Life? And why do I see her as a rag-picker
> on the American cinema, shuffling along wrapped in a filthy shawl
> with her old claws crooked over a stick?
>
> Answer: The direct result of the American cinema acting upon a
> weak mind.[21]

As the story's title suggests, though, in spite of this heightened susceptibility
to influence through the new media of the day, Mansfield is preoccupied
here as elsewhere with the failures of communication which haunt everyday
lives, and which work to constrain women in particular.

Mansfield's stories, like Woolf's, are attentive to women's 'obscure ...
unrecorded lives'. Like Richardson and Woolf (as in Mrs Dalloway's receipt
of the news of Septimus Smith's suicide during her party), she is paradoxically alert to the silence which surrounds and threatens communication,
often with thoughts of death. Several of her major stories explore this issue.
In 'The Garden-Party', the feverishly anticipated social event of the title is
overshadowed (but not put off) by news of the accidental death of a man
from some cottages near the big house at which the party is taking place.
Laura, one of the daughters of the house, is particularly exercised by the
news and, when the party is over, takes a basket of food to the man's family,
where she is shown in to see the body (p. 261):

> He was given up to his dream. What did garden-parties and baskets
> and lace frocks matter to him? He was far from all those things. He
> was wonderful, beautiful. While they were laughing and while the
> band was playing, this marvel had come to the lane.

Upon her return to the house, Laura is overcome when relating the incident
to her brother: '"Isn't life," she stammered, "isn't life –" But what life was
she couldn't explain. No matter. He quite understood. "*Isn't* it, darling?"
said Laurie.' There the story ends, or breaks off. Laurie's 'understanding'
resonates with his incomprehension of what Laura has experienced. His
dismissal reinstates social normality, yet buries the girl's emotional sensitivity
to what has occurred.

In the subsequent story to this in Mansfield's 1922 collection, *The
Garden-Party and Other Stories*, 'The Daughters of the Late Colonel' are
rendered similarly inarticulate once the patriarch who has centred their
lives has died. In a series of short scenes, Mansfield sketches the spinster
daughters' attempts to re-establish the normative rhythms of life. They
reflect upon missed possibilities and, tragically, come to understand that
their lives lived in service of the father had been a lie. The house is
cluttered with relics from the colonel's imperial service, and, standing

before a Buddha, one of the daughters comes to realize the falsity of it all (p. 284):

> There had been this other life, running out, bringing things home in bags, getting things on approval, discussing them with Jug, and taking them back to get more things on approval, and arranging father's trays and trying not to annoy father . . . It wasn't real. It was only when she came out of the tunnel into the moonlight or by the sea or into a thunderstorm that she really felt herself. What did it mean?

This story too ends upon an inability to communicate what it is that has been understood by the experience: 'I've forgotten what it was . . . that I was going to say.' The daughters' belated liberation from the father's influence does not bring greater insight, but rather a further confirmation of the constriction under which they have always lived. The story again breaks off, rather than reaching a conclusion, itself constrained by the demands of the situation it has explored. Mansfield's method in other of her stories is to turn this failure of communication into a scathing comedy on 'modern' relations between the sexes. Works like 'The Honeymoon' and 'Marriage à la Mode' confirm that, even within intimate relations, the capacity for understanding is lacking, and that it is the men who are frequently unable to break through convention to establish true connection.

The tellingly titled 'Psychology', from the slightly earlier collection *Bliss and Other Stories* (1920), stages an encounter between two would-be writers. 'Like two open cities in the midst of some vast plain their minds lay open to each other' (p. 112). The two are articulate when discussing the possibilities of the 'novel of the future' as a psychological one, but unable to express their feelings for each other. As a result, the woman comes to realize the dismalness of her partner as he leaves: 'She saw the beautiful fall of the steps, the dark garden ringed with glittering ivy . . . He was superior to it all. He – with his wonderful "spiritual" vision!' (p. 117). But such is her need for the relationship that in his absence she has to seek to re-establish connection, and dashes off a letter once again on the subject of 'the novel of the future': '"it really is intensely interesting"'. The poignancy of Mansfield's perception of these difficulties is her sense of their inescapability. The fragmented nature of her stories reflects the unresolved modernity of the situations they describe. In her work, as in that of Woolf and Stein, the questions that she asks about former presumptions around gender, individuality, and relationship lead her to put pressure on traditional narrative structures.

In terms of gender, as well as in terms of nationhood, therefore, modernism instilled new and exciting challenges and possibilities. A new awareness of the gendering of space in the modern city, of the exclusions and freedoms it offered, went along with a scepticism towards repressive social mores and an embracing of the freedoms offered by new media amongst women writers. As a result, the constraints of the abiding literary tradition, as well as those of women's everyday lives, were confronted and questioned. Male writers reacted to these innovations with insecurity or outright antagonism. But the political impetus of writing by such women as Woolf, Loy, Mansfield, Wharton, H. D., and Stein changed literary possibility and form for all.

Notes

1 T. S. Eliot, *The Inventions of the March Hare: Poems 1909–1917*, edited by Christopher Ricks (London, 1996), p. 395.
2 Ezra Pound, *Personae*, revised edition by Lea Baechler and A. Walton Litz (New York, 1990), p. 90.
3 *The Literary Essays of Ezra Pound*, edited by T. S. Eliot (London, 1954), p. 295.
4 Wallace Stevens, *The Necessary Angel: Essays on Reality and the Imagination* (London, 1960), pp. 10–11.
5 William Carlos Williams, Imaginations (New York, 1970), p. 95.
6 Roy Foster, *Modern Ireland 1600–1972* (Harmondsworth, 1989), pp. 431–60. The continuing nationalist struggle in Ireland had an emblematic place in defining political disturbance in modernist texts, from Kate Leslie's earlier marriage to an Irish nationalist politician in Lawrence's *The Plumed Serpent* (1926) to the inclusion of Parnell's death in the 1891 section of Woolf's *The Years*.
7 James Joyce, *A Portrait of the Artist as a Young Man*, edited by Seamus Deane (Harmondsworth, 1992), p. 220.
8 James Joyce, *Ulysses*, edited by Jeri Johnson (Oxford, 1993), p. 317.
9 *James Joyce, Occasional, Critical, and Political Writing*, edited by Kevin Barry (Oxford, 2000), pp. 121, 118.
10 Explorations, selected by Mrs Yeats (London, 1962), p. 232.
11 *The Collected Poems of W. B. Yeats*, edited by Richard J. Finneran (Basingstoke, 1989), p. 108.
12 See particularly the story 'Ivy Day in the Committee Room' from *Dubliners*, and the opening chapter of *A Portrait of the Artist as a Young Man*.
13 *The Complete Poems and Plays of T. S. Eliot* (London, 1969), pp. 195, 197.
14 *Lawrence on Hardy and Painting*, edited by J. V. Davis (London, 1973), pp. 16, 18, 41, 53.
15 Virginia Woolf, *A Room of One's Own/Three Guineas*, edited by Michele Barrett (Harmondsworth, 1993), pp. 3, 35.
16 A similar acknowledgement of the necessity for a new kind of writing to open up new kinds of consciousness and new relations between male and female recurs in Woolf's later fiction. The vocal scoring of *The Waves* (1931) deploys an ebb and flow of different mediations to delineate the progression of a group of friends from youth to middle age. It also self-consciously draws our attention to its methodology: '"I love," said Susan, "and I hate." ... "But when we sit together, close," said Bernard, "we melt into each other with phrases. We are edged with mist. We make an unsubstantial territory"' (edited by Kate Flint (Harmondsworth, 2000), p. 10).

17 Gertrude Stein, *Look At Me Now and Here I Am: Writings and Lectures 1911–1945*, edited by Patricia Meyerowitz (London, 1967), p. 21.
18 Edith Wharton, *The House of Mirth*, edited by Martha Banta (Oxford, 1994), pp. 16–17.
19 John Stevenson, *British Society 1914–45* (Harmondsworth, 1994), p. 76.
20 *Close Up 1927–1933: Cinema and Modernism*, edited by James Donald, Anne Friedburg, and Laura Marcus (London, 1998), pp. 160, 176.
21 *The Collected Stories of Katherine Mansfield* (Harmondsworth, 1981), p. 62.

|6|

Has modernism ended?

As the questions around the dates of modernism's 'beginning' and 'ending' raised in Chapter 1 suggest, it is difficult to define a moment at which 'modernism' ceased and 'postmodernism' came into being as a useful distinguishing critical phenomenon. It used to be a critical commonplace that, with the arrival of the seemingly self-contained and definitive literary decade (in Britain at least) of the 1930s, there came a counter-movement to the achievements of the 'high' modernism of the preceding twenty years. Figures like W. H. Auden and George Orwell, with their left-leaning (if non-institutional) politics and their different literary co-ordinates (Charles Dickens, Thomas Hardy), seemed to challenge the ideological and literary-experimental profile of figures like Pound, Eliot, and Woolf. More particularly, the perceived obscurity of much modernist writing, its resistance to mass audience understanding, became anathema to a generation of writers who emerged at the time of social unrest of the mid-1920s. This was a time when the brief General Strike in Britain (1926) set miners and pit-owners, transport workers and managers, against each other. The issue of social class, and of class warfare, which is integral to Lawrence's work, but which only flickers elsewhere in mainstream modernist writing, came to be more predominant in the 1930s.

Yet some recent commentary has sought to challenge this literary map of the first three decades of the twentieth century and beyond.[1] In many obvious ways it is contentious, not least because many of the major works which might be classified as modernist were produced beyond the end of the 1920s. James Joyce's experimentalism was further developed and concentrated in *Finnegan's Wake,* which appeared finally in 1939. W. B. Yeats's *Last Poems,* which includes some of his greatest work ('Long-Legged Fly', 'The Circus Animals' Desertion') appeared in the same year. T. S. Eliot's last major poetry came with *Four Quartets,* not completed until over halfway into World War Two; his experiments with verse drama continued into the 1950s. The epic quest represented by Ezra Pound's *The Cantos* had not been completed at his death in 1972, and instalments had continued to appear into the late 1960s. Virginia Woolf showed a continuing evolution of her work through *The Waves* (1931), *The Years* (1937), and into her last novel, *Between the Acts* (1941). *The Years*, indeed, shows some evidence of a counter-influence from the later generation back towards modernism. This 'novel-essay' tracing social history through several generations from 1880 to the 'Present Day' reflects (however partially) something of the social realism which had been present in the Edwardian fiction of Woolf's youth (Wells, Arnold Bennett). It was certainly a social realism that was re-emerging in the early novels of Orwell like *A Clergyman's Daughter* (1935) and *Keep the Aspidistra Flying* (1936) and, more particularly, in *South Riding* (1936) by Woolf's friend and biographer, Winifred Holtby.

It would not be true to say either that the 'Auden generation' of the 1930s was determined in every way to throw off all facets of the modernist revolution in their work. In terms of their career, for a start, this would have been unwise. T. S. Eliot, as editor at Faber, was responsible for publishing many of that 'generation'; Virginia and Leonard Woolf, through their Hogarth Press, published more. And the ways in which the 1930s' writers appropriated parts of the modernist inheritance to their own ends are sometimes surprising. One of the Auden circle, the Northern Irish poet Louis MacNeice, for instance, pointed out that the kinds of poetic diction deployed by Eliot and (perhaps even more surprisingly) by Yeats, enabled the younger generation to establish their own realistic modernity.[2]

The 1930s also saw the transposition of various 'modernist' techniques to a more intense exposition of different social, gender, and cultural concerns than had been the case in the previous twenty years. Evelyn Waugh's early novels of the decade, including *Vile Bodies* (1930) and *A Handful of Dust* (1934), for instance, adapt the tradition of the English social novel of manners to the seemingly random narration of modernist work. Waugh succeeds through this method in charting the social and moral disintegration of the inter-war generation of decadents. Jean Rhys, born in the West Indies in 1890, produced *Voyage in the Dark* (1934) and *Good Morning, Midnight* (1939). These are works which chart the unfulfilled nature of love and sex, as well as the financial precariousness of modern single women, in ways that are bleaker and more explicit than their precursors in women's fiction from the 1890s onwards. In *Voyage in the Dark*, particularly, Rhys's own mixed cultural background serves to bring a further dimension of disturbance to the metropolitan narrative. At the height of one affair, for instance, the heroine Anna finds her dreams overshadowed by disruptive reminiscence:

'and that hibiscus once – it was so red, so proud, and its long gold tongue hung out ... And I can't believe it's dead.'[3] A similar sense of division between times, countries, and places hangs over the early novels of the Irish writer Samuel Beckett, with their characteristic pitting of their central figure's thoughts and consciousness against the limitations of external reality. This is so from the opening of his first mature novel, *Murphy* (1938): 'The sun shone, having no alternative, on the nothing new. Murphy sat out of it, as though he were free, in a mews in West Brompton.'[4]

In later poetry from Britain, Ireland, and America, which has followed modernist techniques in breaking with traditional form, there has been a similar adaptation to more restricted and local circumstance. David Jones followed his 1937 meditation on the First World War, *In Parenthesis*, with *The Anathémata* in 1952, a densely allusive work on the Eliot model which wove local Cockney and Welsh intonations and allusions into the fabric of a sustained epic. The Scots poet Hugh MacDiarmid's 1955 *In Memoriam James Joyce: From A Vision of World Language* continued the ambition to include the world in a modern work:

> Ah, Joyce, this is our task,
> Making what a moving, thrilling, mystical, tropical,
> Maniacal, magical creation of all these oppositions,
> Of good and evil, greed to self-sacrifice,
> Selfishness to selflessness, of this all-pervading atmosphere,
> Of the seen merging with the unseen,
> Of the beautiful sacrificed to the ugly ...[5]

The Northumbrian poet Basil Bunting, an associate of Pound during his time in Paris and Italy, continued his sequence of so-called poetic 'Sonatas', and produced the last and greatest of them, 'Briggflatts', in the 1960s. 'Briggflatts' interweaves Wordsworthian perceptions of the local landscape with a version of the poet as exile in the modern city of London:

> Secret, solitary, a spy, he gauges
> lines of a Flemish horse
> hauling beer, the angle, obtuse,
> a slut's blouse draws on her chest,
> counts beat against beat, bus conductor
> against engine against wheels against
> the pedal, Tottenham Court Road ...[6]

What each of these subsequent British poets engaging with modernist writing have achieved is, notably, the discovery of a way of accommodating it within a local landscape and perspective: one which includes the metropolis but which centres itself beyond, amidst regional traditions.[7] This drawing upon a variety of traditions, modernist and traditional, within a local context has echoed through the contemporary poet Geoffrey Hill's writing, from at least *Mercian Hymns* (1971), down to *The Orchards of Syon* (2002). Modernism is not a universal concept, but one that gets variously appropriated and retranslated within a variety of historical temporalities depending upon local circumstance. Indeed, it is not something that has ended, since it continues to yield a variety of possibilities depending upon location and cultural context. Pound and Williams, for instance, found perhaps unlikely heirs in Ireland in the late 1950s and 1960s in Thomas Kinsella and John Montague, as the country emerged from decades of cultural, political, and religious conservatism.[8]

This sense that modernism has not proved to have the universal resonance that some of its initial promulgators, including T. S. Eliot, had hoped is never more proven than in subsequent American poetry. Pound's and William Carlos Williams's immediate heirs were the group which gathered at Black Mountain College around Charles Olson. Olson seized upon the dynamism of syntax and imagery in the older poets to develop what in 1950 he called 'Projective Verse' ('A poem is energy transferred from where the poet got it . . . by way of the poem itself to, all the way over to, the reader').[9] Olson is preoccupied as a result with an emphasis upon the kineticism of poetic writing, something he called 'FIELD COMPOSITION': the sense of the poem on the page as a space in which certain energies can be released by language to the ear of the reader. His most elaborate exposition of this theory is in *The Maximus Poems*, which put the present of the New England town of Gloucester into relation with both its own and an international history and literature. Olson's peers such as, most notably, Robert Creeley, have developed 'FIELD COMPOSITION' within much tighter structures relating to the intimacies of domesticity and love.

Many of the dominant themes associated with modernism discussed throughout this book have had an effect, therefore, which has marked literature in English subsequently. These are themes relating to the nature of identity in the modern world; to gender and to sexuality; to the relation between literary technique and contemporary consciousness; to the individual and their relation to history, to myth and belief, to the city and society. At the thematic level, therefore, it might be difficult to distinguish 'modernism' from what has become know as 'postmodernism'. This is the case because 'postmodernism' itself has a dual charge, suggesting both a literary historical period (starting perhaps with the end of the Second World War in 1945), and also a key *theoretical* idea.

As a *theory*, 'postmodernism' signals a range of thought including 'post-structuralism', 'deconstruction', 'feminism', 'queer theory', 'postcolonialism', and several others. A broad definition of 'postmodernism' might suggest that all of these strands have one thing in common. This is the concern to challenge traditional social, cultural, and political hierarchies – the dominant stories of culture – and to suggest that there is no single true way of perceiving the world and mediating it through texts. Seminal essays, like Roland Barthes' 'The Death of the Author', have cast postmodernism as a crisis of meaning. The old balance in terms of religion and gender, and in the power relation between author/god and reader/subject, is destabilized permanently.

But, as my investigations in this book have suggested, many of these issues were central to 'classical' modernism as well. Modernism was also responding to a perceived destruction of former 'civilized' values, narratives of progression, and imperial progress, and also to the spread of democracy and the rise of the women's movement. Under these constraints, many earlier presumptions about literary technique, and the relation of the author to the reader, were destabilized. Traditional narrative hierarchies and poetic lyricism were under threat. 'Postmodernism' as a theoretical phenomenon which entered the discussion of literature in the academy from the late 1960s onwards is, at best, a reprise and further development at a later historical moment (principally around the Vietnam War, student unrest in Paris and America, and a resurgent feminist movement) of some of the concerns which had exercised writers and thinkers from 1900 onwards – concerns given extra impetus by the First World War.

Notes

1   See, for example, *Rewriting the Thirties: Modernism and After*, edited by Keith Williams and Steven Matthews (Harlow, 1997).
2   *Selected Literary Criticism of Louis MacNeice*, edited by Alan Heuser (Oxford, 1987), pp. 156, 191.
3   Jean Rhys, *Voyage in the Dark*, introduced by Carole Angier (Harmondsworth, 2000), p. 49.
4   Samuel Beckett, *Murphy* (London, 1977), p. 5.
5   Hugh MacDiarmid, *The Complete Poems of Hugh MacDiarmid*, vol. 2 (Harmondsworth, 1985), p. 821.
6   Basil Bunting, 'Briggflatts', in *Collected Poems* (Oxford, 1978), p. 43.
7   The so-called 'poetry wars' in Britain have, however, involved a clash between this version of British modernism and one which is more resolutely Poundian, a version which includes the various art of writers such as J. H. Prynne and Allen Fisher.

8 See my *Irish Poetry: Politics, History, Negotiation* (Basingstoke, 1997) for further discussion of this local modernist inheritance.
9 Charles Olson, 'Projective Verse', in *Modern Poets on Modern Poetry*, edited by James Scully (London, 1966), p. 272.

Extracts

1 From May Sinclair, 'The Novels of Dorothy Richardson', *The Egoist*, vol. 4, no. 5 (April 1918)

By imposing very strict limitations upon herself [Richardson] has brought her art, her method, to a high pitch of perfection . . . Obviously, she must not interfere; she must not analyse or comment or explain . . . She must not be the wise, all-knowing author . . . She is not concerned, in the way that other novelists are concerned, with character. Of the person's [sic] who move through [her heroine's] world you know nothing but what [she] knows . . .

To me these three novels show an art and method and form carried to punctilious perfection. Yet I have heard other novelists say that they have no art and no method and no form, and that it is this formlessness that annoys them. They say that they have no beginning and no middle and no end, and that to have form a novel must have an end and a beginning and a middle . . . There is a certain plausibility in what they say, but it depends upon what constitutes a beginning and a middle and an end. In this series there is no drama, no situation, no set scene. Nothing happens. It is just life going on and on. It is [the heroine's] stream of consciousness going on and on . . .

In identifying herself with this life . . . Miss Richardson produces her effect of being the first, of getting closer to reality than any of our novelists who are trying so desperately to get close. No attitude or gesture of her own is allowed to come between her and her effect.

2 From 'The Issues of the War', by C. Grant Robertson, *The New Age* (1 October 1914)

For what does Great Britain and the British Empire stand? Until the war was declared we were the champion in our public diplomatic action of certain clear principles ... In a word, we pleaded and worked for peace, for the rights of small nationalities ... for the sanctity of international covenants. Implicitly we contended that the progress of civilisation was bound up with these principles, and that to abandon or violate them was a deliberate lapse into barbarism and a sacrifice of a century's moral and political travail.

But once we were at war, and at war with Germany, these plain principles became blended in grave and more fundamental issues. The existence of the British Empire as it is at present constituted, the principles upon which that Empire has been built up, the character and aims of our social and political life as an organic whole, the ideals which the British race hope to achieve – these transcended the diplomatic issues ... It is the barest and simplest truth to assert that the fundamental questions for us are these: Is the British Empire going to continue as it is at present constituted or not? Is it going to secure as a result of the war the conditions which alone can enable it to realise the purpose and ideals of its citizens? Consider, therefore, the character of the British State. First, there is the reign of law. By that we broadly mean that our citizens live under and must obey the law, and that our executive and our judiciary are so framed as to secure this. Secondly, the law under which we are all required to live is made and is alterable only by the Crown in Parliament, in which the dominant power is the House of Commons both in legislation and taxation. Thirdly, we have Parliamentary Government ... Fourthly, there is the complete supremacy of the civil power. Englishmen long ago decided that they would not be ruled either by priests or soldiers. The Army and the Navy are executive organs of the civil power ... The four prime features are the essence of our representative self-government – government by the consent of the governed; they are in sharp and complete antithesis to the principles both of the Prussian Constitution and of the Prussianised Federal Constitution of the German Empire.

Furthermore, these essential principles are stamped on the constitutions of the great self-governing parts of the Empire. The Dominion of Canada, the Commonwealth of Australia, the Colonies of New Zealand and Newfoundland, the Union of South Africa, have representative Parliamentary Government.

... Are we not justified in claiming that the fundamental peril to-day is militarism and all its works, and that Germany is the avowed champion of militarism; that the German challenge must be taken up and fought to a finish ... At the bidding of Germany the Angel of Death is abroad through the world ... Let us of the British Empire insist with an icy resolution and an unfaltering faith in our heritage that we will have no peace that does not end, and end for ever, this curse of war. If our generation has not been spared the sorrow and desolation that has fallen on Europe we can at least see that the boys and girls of to-day will grow up to be men and women free from fear and the pollution that militarism has burned into the human race. We owe it to those who will live and to whom the future belongs. It is our duty to the dead. Then, and then only, can we say that they have not died in vain.

3 From W. H. R. Rivers, *Instinct and the Unconscious: A Contribution to a Biological Theory of the Psycho-Neuroses*, Appendix VIII, 'The Instinct of Acquisition' (1920 – but the Appendix is derived from an article of 1916)

A striking example of the difference of attitude [between European and what he calls elsewhere in the book 'savage peoples'] towards common and individual ownership of land was given to me in the island of Mota in the Banks group. Here it was the custom for a man who had cleared a piece of land to mark out an area for the use of each of his children. I worked out the history of a plot of land which had been divided up in this way several generations ago. After the plot had been assigned to each child, the rest was left for the common use of all. Each of the individual plots had passed from one person to another in the course of time and each was still regarded as an individual possession ... [yet] there was never any quarrelling about the use of that part of the original plot which had been left for the common use of the descendants of the original clearer.

I cannot refrain here from pointing out a striking resemblance between this Melanesian example of the ownership of land and the nature of the acquisition of territory by birds of which Howard has given so striking an account. This observer finds that early in the year a flock of birds may be observed living a common life on an area of land. As spring advances individual males leave the flock one after another and acquire individual territories ... [but] part of the original area still continues to be occupied by the rest of the flock ...

It is impossible to ignore the fact that in this Melanesian case of human behaviour we have just such an example of the association of communal ownership with peace and of individual ownership with strife as is presented by bird society.

. . . In the case of man . . . we find that, if man's attitude towards property is determined by an instinct of acquisition, the instinct of different peoples has undergone in such very different degrees the process of modification in response to individual needs. If we suppose that the attitude towards property has an instinctive basis we are driven into the position that this crude individual instinct is far more powerful among ourselves than among the Melanesians, and that it has in far less measure been modified in response to the needs of social life . . .

It is an easy course to reject the value of such comparative study in its relation to our social problems by pointing out that the bird has evolved on lines widely different from our own and that the Melanesian is a palpable failure in the social struggle for existence. Such arguments may have a certain amount of force so long as we treat the problem on purely historical lines and fail to bring psychological explanations to bear on it. But the rejection of such evidence is no longer possible when we turn to psychology for guidance, and seek for the general psychological laws which have guided the evolution of societies.

4 From Mrs Pankhurst's lecture, 'The Importance of the Vote' (delivered 24 March 1908)

What, then, is this vote that we are hearing so much about just now, so much more than people have heard in discussion at least, for a great many years? I think we may give the vote a threefold description. We may describe that vote as, first of all, a symbol, secondly, a safeguard, and thirdly, an instrument. It is a symbol of freedom, a symbol of citizenship, a symbol of liberty. It is a safeguard of all those liberties which it symbolises. And in these later days it has come to be regarded more than anything else as an instrument, something with which you can get a great many more things than our forefathers who fought for the vote ever realised as possible to get with it. It seems to me that such a thing is worth fighting for, and women to-day are fighting very strenuously in order to get it.

Wherever masses of people are gathered together there must be government. Government without the vote is more or less a form of tyranny. Government with the vote is more or less representative according to the extent to which the vote is given. In this country they tell us that we have representative government. So far as women are concerned, while you have representative government for men, you have despotic government for women.

... You saw that a great statesman [Mr John Burns] is going to decide by Act of Parliament whether married women are to be allowed to earn an economic independence, or are to be prevented from doing so. He thinks married women who are earning their living are going to submit to a repeal of the Married Women's Property Act, and to leave it to their husbands to decide whether they shall have any money to spend as they please. To deprive married women of the right to go out to work, to decide this for them without consulting women voters whether they are to earn wages or not, is an act of tyranny to which, I believe, women, patient and long-suffering as they are, will not submit ... Fortunately the women who are going to be interfered with are not the kind of women who will submit to be interfered with quietly. Women who belong to the aristocracy of industry, women such as the cotton workers in the Lancashire mills, are not likely to be driven into the ranks of the sweated without protest.

What is the reason for the proposal? We are told it is to set these women free, to let them stay at home. I do not see that Mr John Burns proposes to compensate women for the loss of their earnings. I do not see that he proposes to compel husbands to give to their wives a definite proportion of their income for house-keeping purposes. All he proposes is that women, who are earning from ten shillings to thirty shillings a week shall be prevented from earning that income for themselves ... This, he says, will stop infantile mortality and put an end to race degeneracy. Could you have a greater example of ignorance of the real facts of the situation? I come from Lancashire. I was born in Lancashire ... I can tell you this, that infantile mortality and physical degeneration are not found in the homes of the well-paid factory operatives, but they are found in the home of the slum-dweller, the home of the casual labourer, where the mother does not go out to work, but where there is never sufficient income to provide proper food for the child after it is born. That is where babies die ...

1890–1930
Timeline of key events and publications

1890   First meeting of the poets' group 'The Rhymer's Club' (–1894)
        Ibsen, *Hedda Gabler*
        Frazer, *The Golden Bough* first volume (12 vols –1915)
1891   Charles Stewart Parnell, Irish Nationalist leader, dies
        Thomas Hardy, *Tess of the D'Urbervilles*
        First London performance of Ibsen's *Ghosts*
1892   Independent Labour Party formed
        Symons, 'The Decadent Movement in Literature'
1895   Marconi invents 'wireless' technology
        Invention of the cinematograph
        Oscar Wilde convicted for committing acts of gross indecency, May
        Conrad, *Almayer's Folly*
1897   Queen Victoria's Diamond Jubilee
        National Union of Women's Suffrage Societies founded, UK
        Stoker, *Dracula*
        Conrad, *The Nigger of the 'Narcissus'*
1898   The Curies discover radium and plutonium
        Symons, *The Symbolist Movement in Literature*
1899   Anglo-Boer War begins
        Conrad, *Heart of Darkness* serialized
1900   Conrad, *Lord Jim*
1901   Queen Victoria dies
1902   Anglo-Boer War ends
        J. A. Hobson, *Imperialism: A Study*
1903   Emmeline Pankhurst founds Women's Social and Political Union
1904   Conrad, *Nostromo*

1905   Albert Einstein proposes the theory of relativity
1906   Liberal Party wins British election
1907   First Cubist Exhibition, Paris
       Conrad, *The Secret Agent*
1908   Feminist protests, Mrs Pankhurst jailed
       Asquith prime minister in Britain
       Ezra Pound arrives in London; Ford Madox Ford edits *The English
       Review*
       Forster, *A Room With a View*
       Stein, *Three Lives*
1909   Royal Commission on Divorce, looking into equal rights for
       women
       Wells, *Ann Veronica*
1910   King Edward VII dies; George V becomes king
       Marinetti first visits London
       'Manet and the Post-Impressionists' at the Grafton Galleries,
       London (–Jan. 1911)
       Forster, *Howards End*
1911   National Insurance Act
       Mansfield, *In a German Pension*
1912   Sinking of the *Titanic*
       Second Post-Impressionist show, London
       First visit of Diaghilev's Russian Ballet to London
       Start of suffragette shop-window breaking campaign
       Insurance Act allows fifteen weeks' support per annum for
       unemployed
1913   London Psychoanalytical Society founded
       First performance of Schoenberg's *Five Pieces for Orchestra* in
       London
       Lawrence, *Sons and Lovers*
1914   First World War begins (August)
       Armory show, New York (17 February–15 March)
       Joyce, *Dubliners*
       Yeats, *Responsibilities*
       Blast published
1915   Zeppelins attack London
       War-time coalition government formed in Britain
       Freud's *The Interpretation of Dreams* published in England (first
       translation of Freud into English)
       Ford, *The Good Soldier*
       Lawrence, *The Rainbow*

1916 Universal conscription introduced in the UK
      Battles of Verdun and the Somme
      Lloyd George becomes prime minister
      Easter Uprising in Dublin, Ireland
      Joyce, *A Portrait of the Artist as a Young Man*
      Pound, *Lustra*

1917 USA enters the war
      Russian Revolution
      Eliot, *Prufrock and Other Observations*
      Yeats, *The Wild Swans at Coole*

1918 Armistice brings end of First World War
      Women granted limited voting rights in the UK

1919 Versailles Treaty
      Non-cooperation protests led by Gandhi, India; Amritsar Massacre
      Woolf, *Night and Day*

1920 League of Nations created
      Nineteenth Amendment to the US Constitution gives women vote
      Lawrence, *Women in Love*
      Mansfield, *Bliss and Other Stories*
      Pound, *Hugh Selwyn Mauberley*

1921 Irish Free State founded

1922 Mussolini comes to power in Italy
      Eliot, *The Waste Land*
      Joyce, *Ulysses*
      Woolf, *Jacob's Room*

1923 Stevens, *Harmonium*

1924 Lenin dies
      Minority Labour government, UK; Ramsay MacDonald prime minister
      Forster, *A Passage to India*

1925 Woolf, *Mrs Dalloway*
      Eliot, *Poems 1909–25*
      Scott Fitzgerald, *The Great Gatsby*

1926 General Strike in UK

1927 Woolf, *To the Lighthouse*

1928 Vote given to women over twenty-one in UK
      Yeats, *The Tower*
      Lawrence, *Lady Chatterley's Lover*

1929 Crash of Wall Street Stock Exchange, New York
      Woolf, *A Room of One's Own*

1930   Civil disobedience movement in India (–1932)
        W. H. Auden, *Poems*
        Waugh, *Vile Bodies*

Suggestions for further reading

General studies of the period

Tim Armstrong, *Modernism, Technology and the Body* (Cambridge, 1998).

Malcolm Bradbury and James McFarlane, eds, *Modernism* (London, 1976).

David Bradshaw, ed., *A Concise Companion to Modernism* (Oxford, 2003).

Christopher Butler, *Early Modernism: Literature, Music and Painting in Europe 1900–1916* (Oxford, 1994).

Lynne Hapgood and Nancy L. Paxton, eds, *Outside Modernism: In Pursuit of the English Novel, 1900–30* (Basingstoke, 2000).

Carola M. Kaplan and Anne B. Simpson, eds, *Seeing Double: Revisioning Edwardian and Modernist Literature* (Basingstoke, 1996).

J. Gerald Kennedy, *Imagining Paris: Exile, Writing and American Identity* (New Haven, 1993).

Michael Levenson, *A Genealogy of Modernism* (Cambridge, 1984).

Michael Levenson, ed., *The Cambridge Companion to Modernism* (Cambridge, 1999).

Peter Nicholls, *Modernisms: A Literary Guide* (Basingstoke, 1995).

Lawrence Rainey, *Institutions of Modernism: Literary Elites and Public Culture* (New Haven, 1998).

Judith Ryan, *The Vanishing Subject: Early Psychology and Literary Modernism* (Chicago, 1991).

Sanford Schwartz, *The Matrix of Modernism: Pound, Eliot, and Early Twentieth-Century Thought* (Princeton, 1985).

Stan Smith, *The Origins of Modernism* (Hemel Hempstead, 1994).

The First World War

Allyson Booth, *Postcards from the Trenches: Negotiating the Space Between Modernism and the First World War* (New York, 1996).

Paul Fussell, *The Great War and Modern Memory* (Oxford, 1975).

Samuel Hynes, *A War Imagined: The First World War and English Culture* (London, 1990).

Arthur Marwick, *The Deluge: British Society and the First World War* (London, 1965).

Trudi Tate, *Modernism, History, and the First World War* (Manchester, 1998).

J. M. Winter, *The First World War and the British People* (Basingstoke, 1985).

Empire, race, and primitivism

Houston A. Baker, Jr, *Modernism and the Harlem Renaissance* (Chicago, 1987).

Elazar Barkan and Ron Bush, eds, *Prehistories of the Future: The Primitivist Project and the Culture of Modernism* (Stanford, 1995).

Michael Bell, *Literature, Modernism and Myth: Belief and Responsibility in the Twentieth Century* (Cambridge, 1998).

Elleke Boehmer, *Colonial and Postcolonial Literature* (Oxford, 1995).

Elleke Boehmer, *Empire, the National, and the Postcolonial 1890–1920* (Oxford, 2002).

Howard J. Booth and Nigel Rigby, eds, *Modernism and Empire* (Manchester, 2000).

Robert Crawford, *The Savage and the City in the Work of T. S. Eliot* (Oxford, 1990).

Michael North, *The Dialect of Modernism: Race, Language, and Twentieth-Century Literature* (New York, 1994).

John P. Vickery, *The Literary Impact of 'The Golden Bough'* (Princeton, 1973).

Gender

Ann L. Ardis, *New Novels: Feminism and Early Modernism* (New Brunswick, 1990).

Shari Benstock, *Women of the Left Bank: Paris 1900–1940* (London, 1987).

Joseph Allen Boone, *Libidinal Currents: Sexuality and the Shaping of Modernism* (Chicago, 1998).

Alice Gambrell, *Women Intellectuals, Modernism and Difference* (Cambridge, 1997).

Sandra M. Gilbert and Susan Gilbar, *No Man's Land: The Place of Woman Writer in the Twentieth Century*, vol. 3 (New Haven, 1994).

Gabriele Griffin, ed., *Difference in View: Women and Modernism* (London, 1994).

Jane Eldridge Miller, *Rebel Women: Feminism, Modernism and the Edwardian Novel* (Alabama, 1997).

Bonnie Kime Scott, ed., *The Gender of Modernism* (Bloomington, 1990).

Modernist publication

Kevin J. H. Dettmar and Stephen Watt, eds, *Marketing Modernisms: Self-Promotion, Canonisation, Re-reading* (Ann Arbor, 1996).

Jayne E. Marek, *'Little' Magazines and Literary History* (Lexington, 1995).

Mark S. Morrisson, *The Public Face of Modernism: Little Magazines, Audiences and Reception, 1905–1920* (Madison, 2001).

Index